P9-DYE-543

The Elephant Man

By Ashley Montagu

MAN'S MOST DANGEROUS MYTH: THE FALLACY OF RACE
THE HUMANIZATION OF MAN
MAN IN PROCESS
HUMAN HEREDITY
THE CULTURED MAN
MAN: HIS FIRST TWO MILLION YEARS
COMING INTO BEING AMONG THE AUSTRALIAN ABORIGINES
EDWARD TYSON, M.D., F.R.S. (1650–1708): AND THE RISE OF HUMAN
    AND COMPARATIVE ANATOMY IN ENGLAND
STATEMENT ON RACE
THE DIRECTION OF HUMAN DEVELOPMENT
THE NATURAL SUPERIORITY OF WOMEN
THE REPRODUCTIVE DEVELOPMENT OF THE FEMALE
ON BEING HUMAN
THE BIOSOCIAL NATURE OF MAN
DARWIN, COMPETITION AND COOPERATION
ON BEING INTELLIGENT
IMMORTALITY, RELIGION, AND MORALS
EDUCATION AND HUMAN RELATIONS
ANTHROPOLOGY AND HUMAN NATURE
INTRODUCTION TO PHYSICAL ANTHROPOLOGY
HANDBOOK OF ANTHROPOMETRY
PRENATAL INFLUENCES
RACE, SCIENCE, AND HUMANITY
LIFE BEFORE BIRTH
THE SCIENCE OF MAN
ANATOMY AND PHYSIOLOGY, 2 VOLS. (WITH E. STEEN)
SEX, MAN, AND SOCIETY
MAN OBSERVED
THE HUMAN REVOLUTION
THE IDEA OF RACE
UP THE IVY
TOUCHING: THE HUMAN SIGNIFICANCE OF THE SKIN
THE AMERICAN WAY OF LIFE
THE ANATOMY OF SWEARING
THE PREVALENCE OF NONSENSE (WITH E. DARLING)
THE IGNORANCE OF CERTAINTY (WITH E. DARLING)
MAN'S EVOLUTION (WITH C. L. BRACE)
TEXTBOOK OF HUMAN GENETICS (WITH M. LEVITAN)
THE DOLPHIN IN HISTORY (WITH JOHN LILLY)

Editor

STUDIES AND ESSAYS IN THE HISTORY OF SCIENCE AND LEARNING
TOYNBEE AND HISTORY
THE MEANING OF LOVE
GENETIC MECHANISMS IN HUMAN DISEASE
INTERNATIONAL PICTORIAL TREASURY OF KNOWLEDGE
ATLAS OF HUMAN ANATOMY
CULTURE AND THE EVOLUTION OF MAN
CULTURE: MAN'S ADAPTIVE DIMENSION
THE CONCEPT OF RACE
THE CONCEPT OF THE PRIMITIVE
MAN AND AGGRESSION
THE HUMAN DIALOGUE (WITH F.E. MATSON)

The Elephant Man

A Study In Human Dignity

by

Ashley Montagu

OUTERBRIDGE & DIENSTFREY

New York
Distributed by E. P. Dutton & Co.

Dedicated to the Memory
of
Charles S. Sonntag

Demonstrator in Human Anatomy
at
University College, London, 1922-1925

Standard Book Number: 0-87690-037-6
Library of Congress Catalog Number: 79-167770
Copyright © 1971 by Ashley Montagu
Copyright: *The Elephant Man and Other Reminiscences*, by Sir
    Frederick Treves: Cassell & Co., Ltd. London
First published in the United States of America in 1971.
Printed in the United States of America.

Design: Ellen Seham
        David E. Seham Associates

Outerbridge & Dienstfrey
200 West 72 Street New York 10023

Contents

List of Illustrations

Preface

It was shortly after its publication, in 1923, that I first read Frederick Treves' *The Elephant Man and Other Reminiscences*. I was immediately fascinated by the title-story. It possessed a special appeal for me, for I was at that time a student of that unlikely combination of subjects, human anatomy and behavior. In addition to the title-story, Treves' other reminiscences circumnavigated an institution, the London Hospital, which, as a boy I had known both intra- and extra-murally for many years. I was thoroughly familiar with the *mise en scène* and, indeed, with almost every place of which Treves wrote. His book dealt with events which had occurred not long before I was born, in a district of London which has always had a strange romantic appeal, and to which the distance of time has added a peculiar enchantment.

For me, then, the book had a threefold appeal: human nature, bones, and the London of Henry Mayhew. The present volume is the result of that combination of interests. It is, first, about two extraordinary men, one a freak of nature, "the Elephant Man," the other a distinguished surgeon and teacher, Frederick Treves. Second, it is about the development of human behavior. And, third, it is about the nature of the astonishing disorder from which "the Elephant Man" suffered. But, I suppose, what the book is finally really about is the triumph of the human spirit over adversity.

I hope the reader will find the book as enthralling as I have in its researching and writing.

In the course of my study of "the Elephant Man" I have been most generously aided by Professor Richard J. Harrison, formerly Professor of Anatomy at the London Hospital Medical College, and now Professor of Anatomy at the University of Cambridge. I owe an especial debt of gratitude to him for his many courtesies, beginning as long ago as 1950. I am also much indebted to the authorities at the London Hospital Medical College for their permission to examine the skeleton and casts of "the Elephant Man," and for the pains they have taken in making most of the photographs for me which illustrate this volume. To Mr. E. P. Entract, Librarian of the London Hospital Medical College, I owe thanks for the photographs of the Hospital and of the College. To the American Medical Association and Dr. Lawrence M. Solomon I am obliged for permission to reprint his essay on "Quasimodo's Diagnosis" as Appendix 11.

For permission to reprint the title-story from *The Elephant Man and Other Reminiscences*, I am obliged to Messrs. Cassell & Co., Ltd. of London.

Finally, I am most grateful to the Librarians of the College of Physicians of Philadelphia, and of Princeton University, for their many kind offices.

Ashley Montagu
Princeton, New Jersey.

Chapter 1

Introduction

Life, like a dome of many-coloured glass,
Stains the white radiance of Eternity,
Until Death tramples it to fragments.

Shelley, *Adonais*

What is a human life? A pulse in the heartbeat of eternity? A cry that begins with birth and ends with death? A brief and tempestuous sojourn on an inhospitable shore, where there is really neither joy, nor love, nor light, nor certitude, nor peace, nor help for pain? Or is it, is it, something more?

In this book, I think, lies something of the answer to these questions. It is a true story. It happened in the eighties of the last century. It is from many angles of vision an enthralling and ennobling story. It tells us something not only about the darker but also about the brighter sides of human nature, of the spontaneous kindness to which human beings are disposed, as well as the unfeeling cruelty of which others are capable, but above all else of the supreme human integrity which some members of the species *Homo sapiens* are able to maintain in the face of never-ending adversities of the most devastating kinds.

The hero of this story, "the Elephant Man," whose real name was John Merrick, lived only twenty-seven years, most of them spent in a living purgatory. Hideously deformed, malodorous, for the most part maltreated, constantly in pain, lame, fed the merest scraps, exhibited as a grotesque monster at circuses, fairs, and wherever else a penny might be turned, the object of constant expressions of horror and disgust, it might have been expected that "the Elephant Man" would have grown into a creature detesting all human beings, bitter, awkward, difficult in his relations with others, ungentle, unfeeling, aggressive, and unlovable.

According to modern psychological theory and observation the socially deprived infant of any species, but especially of the human species, is likely to suffer serious shortcomings in the development of his ability to relate socially toward others. By social deprivation is meant the absence of social stimulations that are necessary for the healthy development of an infant organism: the kinds of stimulations that an attentive mother is likely to give her young. The satisfaction of the need to be touched and to touch others, to be held, cuddled, cooed to, looked at and fed with affection, supported and sustained with love, these are the primary needs that must be satisfied if the infant is to learn to interact adequately with others. The vulnerability of the human infant to maternal neglect particularly, is today attested by innumerable independent studies. As we shall see, "the Elephant Man" seems

unaccountably to have escaped the blight that usually so
seriously befalls the deprived and disadvantaged child. It is
this that makes his story, tragic as it is, so doubly
fascinating and heartening. Before, however, we proceed
with our inquiry into that heroic journey into the night,
the story itself must be told. This is best done in the words
of "the Elephant Man's" benefactor and liberator, Frederick Treves, but for whose compassion and devotion the
world would probably never have heard of John Merrick.
In a very real sense, this is as much Frederick Treves' story
as it is John Merrick's. And so, let us turn to a brief
account of Frederick Treves.

Frederick Treves

Frederick Treves came of old yeomen stock native to
Dorset for centuries. Treves was born at Dorchester,
Dorset, 15 February 1853, the youngest son of William
Treves, an upholsterer, by his wife Jane, daughter of John
Knight of Honiton, some thirty miles northwest of
Dorchester. At the age of seven Treves was sent to the
school kept by the Dorset poet, the Reverend William
Barnes (1801-1886). Barnes, who had commenced school-
mastering in 1822 after his graduation from Cambridge,
was a man of extraordinary genius. Among his many
accomplishments were those of engraver, musician, natu-
ralist, linguist, philologist, humanist, educator, and poet.
His bucolic, often very moving, poems, published in a
series of three volumes, *Poems of Rural Life in the Dorset
Dialect,* between the years 1844 and 1862, had made him
well known to the reading public, but were scarcely

rewarded enough to free him from the poverty and
financial worries which haunted him during the greater
part of his life. Thomas Hardy edited a selection of his
poems which was published in 1908. Barnes has been
described as England's best ecloguist. Perhaps no better
description of the quality of his poetry has been given than
that by Llewelyn Powys. "No poet in all English literature
has done more to reveal the quality of homely village days
as they follow, one after the other, against their background of the fugitive, recurring senses. These bucolic
poems, so innocent and so sturdy, instruct us how to
become accessible to the wonder latent in every mode of
natural existence, teach us to be grateful for the privilege
of life on its simplest terms, with firm purpose and serene
minds, to face our inevitable lot of sorrow and death."[1]

Many collections of Barnes' poems have been published,
and monographs have been written on him in his roles as
poet, philologist, and educator. In all these roles he
excelled. As an educator he was many years ahead of his
time, teaching with love and affection. His chief means of
instruction consisted of discourses delivered as he walked
up and down the room. His favorite subjects were logic
and grammar, and on Treves' first day at school the subject
was "Logic is the Art of the Right Use of Reason." Quite
mystifying to a boy of seven, but unforgettable. Treves to
the end of his life carried with him the singular little
pocket grammar that Barnes published for the benefit of
his class.

It has been said that the greatest gift a teacher can
make to his students is his own personality. In this Barnes
seems to have richly succeeded with his impressionable
young student, as he did with many others. Treves never
forgot the qualities of kindness and understanding of his
teacher, and in his own relations with students and

patients in later life he never failed to exhibit the same traits. In his book *Highways and Byeways of Dorset* (London: Macmillan & Co., 1906), and in his essay "William Barnes, the Dorset Poet" (London: *The Dorset Yearbook, 1915-1916*), Treves has written of his years at school with love and admiration for his old schoolmaster, "a genius whom few recognized." It is evident that Treves' love of literature and his fondness for words were first aroused and developed under the charismatic influence of Barnes. Perhaps the best evidence of these interests is Treves' book, *The Country of "The Ring and the Book,"* published in 1913. The hundred photographs in this book were taken by Treves about the actual date in the calendar on which the episode occurred with which the particular scene was associated.

In his youth Treves was an athlete, a great swimmer who loved the water, subsequently becoming a master of sailing and a qualified mariner.

In 1864 Treves entered Merchant Taylors School in London. Following the completion of his studies there he went on to University College, University of London, and in 1871, at the age of eighteen, he entered upon the study of medicine at the London Hospital. In 1874 he passed the examinations for the Licensure of Apothecaries Hall, and in the following year he successfully completed the examinations for the Membership of the Royal College of Surgeons. In the same year, 1875, he became house-surgeon at the London Hospital, and in 1876 he took up a post as resident medical officer at the Royal National Hospital for Scrofula at Margate, on the south coast, a hospital to which his elder brother William, his senior by ten years, was honorary surgeon. From his experience here and from later continuing research came Treves' first book, *Scrofula and Its Gland Diseases*, published in 1882, the very year in which Robert Koch showed that the disease was due to a bacillus.

Earlier, in 1877, at the age of twenty-four, the year after he became resident medical officer at Margate, Treves married Anne Elizabeth, youngest daughter of Alfred Samuel Mason of Dorchester, and went into practice at Wirksworth, Derbyshire. In the following year Treves took the Fellowship of the Royal College of Surgeons. In 1879 he gave up general practice to assume the surgical registrarship at the London Hospital. He was appointed assistant-surgeon in the same year, and became full surgeon in 1884. (This was the year he was to meet "the Elephant Man" for the first time.) He was also appointed a demonstrator in anatomy at the London Hospital Medical College, and was in charge of the practical teaching of anatomy from 1881 to 1884, when he became lecturer, a post he held until 1893. In the latter year he resigned the lectureship in anatomy to become lecturer in surgery, a post in which he continued till 1897.[2]

In 1883 he published what became his most popular and most widely used book, *Surgical Applied Anatomy*. This went into many editions, and for over half a century served students and surgeons all over the world as the best and most authoritative work on the subject. In 1885, enlarging upon an interest which he had early developed, Treves published a small book on the *Influence of Clothing Upon Health,* in which he discussed the many undesirable features of women's clothing, such as corsetting and tight lacing, including much that was anticipatory of the changes that women have come to make.

In the Medical College Treves soon came to be the outstanding personality of his day. An excellent teacher and surgical operator, he was very popular with the students and came to be the first President of the Students

Figure 1, Sir Frederick Treves (from the Painting by Sir Luke Fildes in the London Hospital Medical College).

Figure 2, Main Front of the London Hospital from the South Side of Whitechapel Road from a Photograph Taken in 1970.

THE HOSPITAL IN THE EIGHTIES

Figure 3, The London Hospital in the Eighties (from a Contemporary Line Drawing, Courtesy of the London Hospital Medical College).

Figure 4, The London Hospital Medical College.

RIGHT, THE NEW NURSES' HOME; LEFT, THE NEW LIBRARY AND, BOTTOM, THE NEW MEDICAL COLLEGE

(From *The Illustrated London News*)

Union, an organization which he helped to found. Good-natured and cheerful, he was renowned for his ability to tell a story well, was hailed as a good companion, and known to his friends as "Freddie."[3]

During this period Treves' practice as a consulting surgeon grew apace. His consulting room at 6 Wimpole Street became one of the best known in England. In 1898, at the age of forty-five, Treves resigned his lectureship in surgery at the hospital to devote full time to his increasingly lucrative surgical practice. (At his death, twenty-five years later, Treves left an estate valued over £100,000.)

Treves' patients were mainly drawn from the wealthy, high society, the nobility, and the Royal Family. His rooms at Wimpole Street were so crowded that he used to put his patients in every available room in the house while they were waiting to be seen by him. Lady Treves used to say that the only room she had to herself was her bedroom. Treves received the hundred guinea fee, then the upper limit for a surgeon, more often than any other surgeon of his day. But even as the leading and busiest surgeon of his day Treves never forgot his poor patients. On Sundays, his only free day, he regularly attended the hospital to examine the cases in his wards more thoroughly and at greater leisure than was possible during weekdays when students and visitors required much of his attention at the bedside. Following the completion of his rounds he would go for a forty- or fifty-mile bicycle ride.

In 1900 Treves was appointed Surgeon-Extraordinary to Queen Victoria. He also became Surgeon-in-Ordinary to the Duke of York, and later Sergeant Surgeon to King George V, and Surgeon-in-Ordinary to Queen Alexandra. He was made a Commander of the Bath, and in 1901 Knight Commander of the Victorian Order. During all this time Treves was busily engaged in producing books and monographs on surgical anatomy, operative procedures, and on intestinal disorders. It was, therefore, natural that when just before his coronation in January 1902, King Edward VII fell ill with an intestinal disorder, Treves should have been called in. In the presence of Lord Lister and Sir Thomas Smith, Treves confirmed the diagnosis as acute appendicitis, a condition which at that time was called perityphlitis, and upon which Treves was the leading surgical authority. Treves advised immediate operation. To this, the King, however, objected. He was determined to go on with his coronation on the 26th of January rather than disappoint the nation. "In that case, Sir," Treves is reported to have said, "you will go to the Abbey as a corpse." After a scene of prolonged and painful pleading the King was ultimately persuaded. Treves successfully operated on him on the day on which he was to have been crowned. That year Treves was created a Baronet and promoted to Grand Commander of the Victorian Order.

In 1906 Treves was elected Lord Rector of the University of Aberdeen. This honor required no more than a single address on the appointed day. Treves happily accepted the invitation, but on condition that the traditional student interruptions be omitted. On the occasion of the Rectorial Address it was the tradition among students to punctuate the oration with appropriate expressions of approval or disapproval by handclapping, footstamping, and vocal inadvertencies. Treves delivered his lecture, and so great was the respect in which he was held by the students that there was, in fact, not a single interruption during the whole hour of his address.

Treves held that after fifty-five no surgeon should operate, and so at that age he retired in 1908 from the active practice of surgery to live in Thatched House Lodge in Richmond Park. This house was lent him by King Edward, with whom he remained on terms of close and confidential friendship, a friendship that was continued with his son King George V. In the following years Treves and his wife traveled widely, in the West Indies, Palestine, the Uganda, and many other places. These travels resulted in a series of books. Lady Treves said that her husband was never happier than when he had a pen in his hand. The truth was that his real love was literature. This is very evident from his various writings. Even his technical works were most elegantly written.

After the 1914-18 war, during which Treves had served as President of the Headquarters Medical Board at the War Office, and was actively engaged in the work of the International Red Cross, sudden heart attacks began to afflict this splendid man. Continuing failing health compelled him to move abroad in 1920, first at Evian on the Savoy side of Lake Geneva. It was here that Treves wrote *The Riviera of the Corniche Road* (1921), *The Lake Geneva* (1922), and his last book *The Elephant Man and Other Reminiscences* (1923). In 1922 Treves suffered a severe attack of pneumonia, from which he seemed to recover. *The Elephant Man* appeared at the beginning of February 1923, and was widely and well reviewed. In the autumn of the same year Treves moved into an apartment at Vevey on the Swiss side of Lake Geneva. There he was taken ill on the 3rd of December with peritonitis. He was quickly removed to a nursing home in Lausanne, but it was too late to do anything, and on 7 December 1923 he died. He was cremated, and his ashes were buried in Dorchester cemetery, his friend Thomas Hardy being present at the ceremony.

Treves had two daughters, the younger of whom predeceased him, dying tragically following an operation for the very disease on which Treves was the world's leading surgical authority, acute appendicitis. Dying without male issue the baronetcy that had been conferred on Treves became extinct.

The Discovery Of "The Elephant Man"

At the time of his discovery of "the Elephant Man" in November 1884 Treves was thirty-one years of age, lecturer in anatomy and surgeon at the London Hospital and the London Hospital Medical College. The London Hospital was the largest institution of its kind in the British Empire, occupying a site of many acres in the middle of the poverty-stricken center of the East End of London. The hospital is situated in Whitechapel Road, a wide and commodious thoroughfare built by the Romans, and running all the way from Aldgate to Cambridge Heath Road, where Whitechapel Road ends and Mile End Road begins. Both roads are said to be the widest in London. Whitechapel takes its name from the white walls of the chapel of ease of the medieval church of St. Mary Matfellon, which had stood on the site of the now World War II bomb-destroyed church of St. Mary in Whitechapel High Street, toward Aldgate. Almost at the juncture of Whitechapel and Mile End Road, on the north side of the latter stands a small rebuilt brick building, which now houses a tobacconist's shop, on the site of which an earlier house stood in which Captain Cook once lived. The original house was destroyed in the German air-raids of 1940, and the plaque it once bore marking the residence of the great navigator was destroyed with it and never restored.

The London Hospital was founded in 1740 and its main building was erected in 1759. The principal buildings are situated on the south side of Whitechapel Road. The London Hospital Medical College, which enjoys the distinction of being the first medical college to be established in association with a hospital upon the model of the faculty of a university, stands on the west side of the main building on Turner Street, opposite the large church of St. Philip. This latter edifice was erected at the expense of one of its vicars, the Reverend Sidney Vatcher, on the site of a church which had dated from 1818. St. Philip church will figure later in our story.

Because of its situation in the midst of the slums of London, in "the roughest and most unsavory part of the town," as Treves himself described it, its more than eight hundred beds, its enormous number of inpatients and still greater number of outpatients, "The London," as it came to be called, had a great appeal from the first for intending students of medicine and medical men of every description. Here could be seen every possible kind of disease and disorder. The experience one could gain at "The London" could scarcely be equalled anywhere else in the world.[4] It was the knowledge of this fact that probably brought the young Frederick Treves to the London Hospital. (By some peculiar lapse of memory Treves places the hospital, at the beginning of his story about "the Elephant Man," in Mile End Road. It is in fact, and has always been, situated in Whitechapel Road.)

On both the north and south sides of Whitechapel Road the pavements, like the cobbled road, are unusually ample, and give support to innumerable small shops. In spite of the bombings of two World Wars, fires, demolitions, rebuilding, and the replacement of horsedrawn vehicles by motor-driven traffic, the appearance of the area remains little changed from what it was in Treves' days at "The London."

During weekdays, and especially on Saturdays, the north side of the road, affords on its ample pavements accomodation for the most colorful of markets. The market extends all the way into Mile End Road. Movable wheelbarrows and stalls by the dozen offer everything for sale from apples and secondhand books to zithers and zippers. From early times the broad expanse of White-chapel Road also had served as a hay market, but with the increase and hazards of motor traffic the market was finally discontinued in 1928.

In Treves' day Whitechapel Road presented a rather more squalid appearance than it does today. The small, neglected shops were a great deal more dingy, and lit by gaslight were dismally uninviting. The poor and abandoned were very much more in evidence, and owing to the poverty of the people, shopkeepers, eking out a precarious living, tended to go out of business with discouraging regularity. The empty shops would stand unrented for months, sometimes years, padlocked, shuttered, dirty, and decaying. Signs in shop windows reading "This Shop to Let" were a common sight. Sometimes a shop would be rented for a short time by a wandering gypsy fortune-teller or an itinerant showman, and as quickly be vacated again. It was in one such vacant greengrocer's shop on an afternoon late in November 1884 that Frederick Treves first came upon "the Elephant Man."

And here we may leave him to tell the story in his own words.

Chapter 2

The Elephant Man
By Sir Frederick Treves

In the Mile End Road, opposite to the London Hospital, there was (and possibly still is) a line of small shops. Among them was a vacant greengrocer's which was to let. The whole of the front of the shop, with the exception of the door, was hidden by a hanging sheet of canvas on which was the announcement that the Elephant Man was to be seen within and that the price of admission was twopence. Painted on the canvas in primitive colors was a life-size portrait of the Elephant Man. This very crude production depicted a frightful creature that could only have been possible in a nightmare. It was the figure of a man with the characteristics of an elephant. The transfiguration was not far advanced. There was still more of the man than of the beast. This fact—that it was still human—was the most repellent attribute of the creature. There was nothing about it of the pitiableness of the misshapened or the deformed, nothing of the grotesqueness of the freak, but merely the loathing insinuation of a man being changed into an animal. Some palm trees in the background of the picture suggested a jungle and might have led the imaginative to assume that it was in this wild that the perverted object had roamed.

When I first became aware of this phenomenon the exhibition was closed, but a well-informed boy sought the proprietor in a public house and I was granted a private view on payment of a shilling. The shop was empty and grey with dust. Some old tins and a few shrivelled potatoes occupied a shelf and some vague vegetable refuse the window. The light in the place was dim, being obscured by the painted placard outside. The far end of the shop—where I expect the late proprietor sat at a desk—was cut off by a curtain or rather by a red tablecloth suspended from a cord by a few rings. The room was cold and dank, for it was the month of November. The year, I might say, was 1884.

The showman pulled back the curtain and revealed a bent figure crouching on a stool and covered by a brown blanket. In front of it, on a tripod, was a large brick heated by a Bunsen burner. Over this the creature was huddled to warm itself. It never moved when the curtain was drawn back. Locked up in an empty shop and lit by the faint blue light of the gas jet, this hunched-up figure was the embodiment of loneliness. It might have been a captive in a cavern or a wizard watching for unholy manifestations in the ghostly flame. Outside the sun was shining and one could hear the footsteps of the passers-by, a tune whistled by a boy and the companionable hum of traffic in the road.

The showman—speaking as if to a dog—called out harshly: "Stand up!" The thing arose slowly and let the blanket that covered its head and back fall to the ground. There stood revealed the most disgusting specimen of humanity that I have ever seen. In the course of my profession I had come upon lamentable deformities of the face due to injury or disease, as well as mutilations and contortions of the body depending upon like causes; but at no time had I met with such a degraded or perverted version of a human being as this lone figure displayed. He was naked to the waist, his feet were bare, he wore a pair of threadbare trousers that had once belonged to some fat gentleman's dress suit.

From the intensified painting in the street I had imagined the Elephant Man to be of gigantic size. This, however, was a little man below the average height and made to look shorter by the bowing of his back. The most striking feature about him was his enormous and mis-shapened head. From the brow there projected a huge bony mass like a loaf, while from the back of the head hung a bag of spongy, fungous-looking skin, the surface of which was comparable to brown cauliflower. On the top of the skull were a few long lank hairs. The osseous growth on the forehead almost occluded one eye. The circumfer-ence of the head was no less than that of the man's waist. From the upper jaw there projected another mass of bone. It protruded from the mouth like a pink stump, turning the upper lip inside out and making of the mouth a mere slobbering aperture. This growth from the jaw had been so exaggerated in the painting as to appear to be a rudimen-tary trunk or tusk. The nose was merely a lump of flesh, only recognizable as a nose from its position. The face was no more capable of expression than a block of gnarled wood. The back was horrible, because from it hung, as far down as the middle of the thigh, huge, sack-like masses of flesh covered by the same loathsome cauliflower skin.

The right arm was of enormous size and shapeless. It suggested the limb of the subject of elephantiasis. It was overgrown also with pendent masses of the same cauliflower-like skin. The hand was large and clumsy—a fin or paddle rather than a hand. There was no distinction between the palm and the back. The thumb had the appearance of a radish, while the fingers might have been thick, tuberous roots. As a limb it was almost useless. The other arm was remarkable by contrast. It was not only normal but was, moreover, a delicately shaped limb covered with fine skin and provided with a beautiful hand which any woman might have envied. From the chest hung a bag of the same repulsive flesh. It was like a dewlap suspended from the neck of a lizard. The lower limbs had the characters of the deformed arm. They were unwieldy, dropsical looking and grossly misshapen.

To add a further burden to his trouble the wretched man, when a boy, developed hip disease, which had left him permanently lame, so that he could only walk with a stick. He was thus denied all means of escape from his tormentors. As he told me later, he could never run away. One other feature must be mentioned to emphasize his isolation from his kind. Although he was already repellent enough, there arose from the fungous skin-growth with which he was almost covered a very sickening stench which was hard to tolerate. From the showman I learnt nothing about the Elephant Man, except that he was English, that his name was John Merrick and that he was twenty-one years of age.

As at the time of my discovery of the Elephant Man I was the Lecturer on Anatomy at the Medical College opposite, I was anxious to examine him in detail and to

prepare an account of his abnormalities. I therefore
arranged with the showman that I should interview his
strange exhibit in my room at the college. I became at
once conscious of a difficulty. The Elephant Man could
not show himself in the streets. He would have been
mobbed by the crowd and seized by the police. He was, in
fact, as secluded from the world as the Man with the Iron
Mask. He had, however, a disguise, although it was almost
as startling as he was himself. It consisted of a long black
cloak which reached to the ground. Whence the cloak had
been obtained I cannot imagine. I had only seen such a
garment on the stage wrapped about the figure of a
Venetian bravo. The recluse was provided with a pair of
bag-like slippers in which to hide his deformed feet. On his
head was a cap of a kind that never before was seen. [*] It
was black like the cloak, had a wide peak, and the general
outline of a yachting cap. As the circumference of
Merrick's head was that of a man's waist, the size of this
head-gear may be imagined. From the attachment of the
peak a grey flannel curtain hung in front of the face. In
this mask was cut a wide horizontal slit through which the
wearer could look out. This costume, worn by a bent man
hobbling along with a stick, is probably the most remarkable and the most uncanny that has as yet been designed. I
arranged that Merrick should cross the road in a cab, and
to insure his immediate admission to the college I gave him
my card. This card was destined to play a critical part in
Merrick's life.

I made a careful examination of my visitor the result of
which I embodied in a paper.[1]   I made little of the man

_____

[*See fig. 5, *A.M.*]

[1]*British Medical Journal,* Dec., 1886, and April, 1890. [See Appendices 5 and
8. *A.M.]*

himself. He was shy, confused, not a little frightened and evidently much cowed. Moreover, his speech was almost unintelligible. The great bony mass that projected from his mouth blurred his utterance and made the articulation of certain words impossible. He returned in a cab to the place of exhibition, and I assumed that I had seen the last of him, especially as I found next day that the show had been forbidden by the police and that the shop was empty.

I supposed that Merrick was imbecile and had been imbecile from birth. The fact that his face was incapable of expression, that his speech was a mere spluttering and his attitude that of one whose mind was void of all emotions and concerns gave grounds for this belief. The conviction was no doubt encouraged by the hope that his intellect was the blank I imagined it to be. That he could appreciate his position was unthinkable. Here was a man in the heyday of youth who was so vilely deformed that everyone he met confronted him with a look of horror and disgust. He was taken about the country to be exhibited as a monstrosity and an object of loathing. He was shunned like a leper, housed like a wild beast, and got his only view of the world from a peephole in a showman's cart. He was, moreover, lame, had but one available arm, and could hardly make his utterances understood. It was not until I came to know that Merrick was highly intelligent, that he possessed an acute sensibility and—worse than all—a romantic imagination that I realized the overwhleming tragedy of his life.

The episode of the Elephant Man was, I imagined, closed; but I was fated to meet him again—two years later—under more dramatic conditions. In England the showman and Merrick had been moved on from place to place by the police, who considered the exhibition degrading and among the things that could not be allowed.

It was hoped that in the uncritical retreats of Mile End a
more abiding peace would be found. But it was not to be.
The official mind there, as elsewhere, very properly
decreed that the public exposure of Merrick and his
deformities transgressed the limits of decency. The show
must close.

The showman, in despair, fled with his charge to the
Continent. Whither he roamed at first I do not know, but
he came finally to Brussels. His reception was discouraging.
Brussels was firm; the exhibition was banned; it was brutal,
indecent and immoral, and could not be permitted within
the confines of Belgium. Merrick was thus no longer of
value. He was no longer a source of profitable entertain-
ment. He was a burden. He must be got rid of. The
elimination of Merrick was a simple matter. He could offer
no resistance. He was as docile as a sick sheep. The
impresario, having robbed Merrick of his paltry savings,
gave him a ticket to London, saw him into the train and no
doubt in parting condemned him to perdition.

His destination was Liverpool Street. The journey may
be imagined. Merrick was in his alarming outdoor garb. He
would be harried by an eager mob as he hobbled along the
quay. They would run ahead to get a look at him. They
would lift the hem of his cloak to peep at his body. He
would try to hide in the train or in some dark corner of
the boat, but never could he be free from that ring of
curious eyes or from those whispers of fright and aversion.
He had but a few shillings in his pocket and nothing either
to eat or drink on the way. A panic-dazed dog with a label
on his collar would have received some sympathy and
possibly some kindness. Merrick received none.

What was he to do when he reached London? He had not
a friend in the world. He knew no more of London than he
knew of Peking. How could he find a lodging, or what

lodging-house keeper would dream of taking him in? All he wanted was to hide. What most he dreaded were the open street and the gaze of his fellow-men. If even he crept into a cellar the horrid eyes and the still more dreaded whispers would follow him to its depths. Was there ever such a homecoming!

At Liverpool Street he was rescued from the crowd by the police and taken into the third-class waiting-room. Here he sank on the floor in the darkest corner. The police were at a loss what to do with him. They had dealt with strange and mouldy tramps, but never with such an object as this. He could not explain himself. His speech was so maimed that he might as well have spoken in Arabic. He had, however, something with him which he produced with a ray of hope. It was my card.

The card simplified matters. It made it evident that this curious creature had an acquaintance and that the individual must be sent for. A messenger was dispatched to the London Hospital which is comparatively near at hand. Fortunately I was in the building and returned at once with the messenger to the station. In the waiting-room I had some difficulty in making a way through the crowd, but there, on the floor in the corner, was Merrick. He looked a mere heap. It seemed as if he had been thrown there like a bundle. He was so huddled up and so helpless looking that he might have had both his arms and his legs broken. He seemed pleased to see me, but he was nearly done. The journey and want of food had reduced him to the last stage of exhaustion. The police kindly helped him into a cab, and I drove him at once to the hospital. He appeared to be content, for he fell asleep almost as soon as he was seated and slept to the journey's end. He never said a word, but seemed to be satisfied that all was well.

In the attics of the hospital was an isolation ward with a

single bed. It was used for emergency purposes—for a case of delirium tremens, for a man who had become suddenly insane or for a patient with an undetermined fever. Here the Elephant Man was deposited on a bed, was made comfortable and was supplied with food. I had been guilty of an irregularity in admitting such a case, for the hospital was neither a refuge nor a home for incurables. Chronic cases were not accepted, but only those requiring active treatment, and Merrick was not in need of such treatment. I applied to the sympathetic chairman of the committee, Mr. Carr Gomm, who not only was good enough to approve my action but who agreed with me that Merrick must not again be turned out into the world.

Mr. Carr Gomm wrote a letter to *The Times* detailing the circumstances of the refugee and asking for money for his support.[*] So generous is the English public that in a few days—I think in a week—enough money was forthcoming to maintain Merrick for life without any charge upon the hospital funds. There chanced to be two empty rooms at the back of the hospital which were little used. They were on the ground floor, were out of the way, and opened upon a large courtyard called Bedstead Square, because here the iron beds were marshalled for cleaning and painting. The front room was converted into a bed-sitting room and the smaller chamber into a bathroom. The condition of Merrick's skin rendered a bath at least once a day a necessity, and I might here mention that with the use of the bath the unpleasant odor to which I have referred ceased to be noticeable. Merrick took up his abode in the hospital in December 1886.

[*See Appendix 4, *A.M.*]

Merrick had now something he had never dreamed of, never supposed to be possible—a home of his own for life. I at once began to make myself acquainted with him and to endeavor to understand his mentality. It was a study of much interest. I very soon learned his speech so that I could talk freely with him. This afforded him great satisfaction, for, curiously enough, he had a passion for conversation, yet all his life had had no one to talk to. I—having then much leisure—saw him almost every day, and made a point of spending some two hours with him every Sunday morning when he would chatter almost without ceasing. It was unreasonable to expect one nurse to attend to him continuously, but there was no lack of temporary volunteers. As they did not all acquire his speech it came about that I had occasionally to act as an interpreter.

I found Merrick, as I have said, remarkably intelligent. He had learned to read and had become a most voracious reader. I think he had been taught when he was in hospital with his diseased hip. His range of books was limited. The Bible and Prayer Book he knew intimately, but he had subsisted for the most part upon newspapers, or rather upon such fragments of old journals as he had chanced to pick up. He had read a few stories and some elementary lesson books, but the delight of his life was a romance, especially a love romance. These tales were very real to him, as real as any narrative in the Bible, so that he would tell them to me as incidents in the lives of people who had lived. In his outlook upon the world he was a child, yet a child with some of the tempestuous feelings of a man. He was an elemental being, so primitive that he might have spent the twenty-three years of his life immured in a cave.

Of his early days I could learn but little. He was very loath to talk about the past. It was a nightmare, the

shudder of which was still upon him. He was born, he believed, in or about Leicester. Of his father he knew absolutely nothing. Of his mother he had some memory. It was very faint and had, I think, been elaborated in his mind into something definite. Mothers figured in the tales he had read, and he wanted his mother to be one of those comfortable lullaby-singing persons who are so lovable. In his subconscious mind there was apparently a germ of recollection in which someone figured who had been kind to him. He clung to this conception and made it more real by invention, for since the day when he could toddle no one had been kind to him. As an infant he must have been repellent, although his deformities did not become gross until he had attained his full stature.

It was a favorite belief of his that his mother was beautiful. The fiction was, I am aware, one of his own making, but it was a great joy to him. His mother, lovely as she may have been, basely deserted him when he was very small, so small that his earliest clear memories were of the workhouse to which he had been taken. Worthless and inhuman as this mother was, he spoke of her with pride and even with reverence. Once, when referring to his own appearance, he said: "It *is* very strange, for, you see, mother was so beautiful."

The rest of Merrick's life up to the time that I met him at Liverpool Street Station was one dull record of degradation and squalor. He was dragged from town to town and from fair to fair as if he were a strange beast in a cage. A dozen times a day he would have to expose his nakedness and his piteous deformities before a gaping crowd who greeted him with such mutterings as "Oh! what a horror! What a beast!" He had had no childhood. He had had no boyhood. He had never experienced pleasure. He knew nothing of the joy of living nor of the fun of things.

His sole idea of happiness was to creep into the dark and hide. Shut up alone in a booth, awaiting the next exhibition, how mocking must have sounded the laughter and merriment of the boys and girls outside who were enjoying the "fun of the fair!" He had no past to look back upon and no future to look forward to. At the age of twenty he was a creature without hope. There was nothing in front of him but a vista of caravans creeping along a road, of rows of glaring show tents and of circles of staring eyes with, at the end, the spectacle of a broken man in a poor law infirmary.

Those who are interested in the evolution of character might speculate as to the effect of this brutish life upon a sensitive and intelligent man. It would be reasonable to surmise that he would become a spiteful and malignant misanthrope, swollen with venom and filled with hatred of his fellow-men, or, on the other hand, that he would degenerate into a despairing melancholic on the verge of idiocy. Merrick, however, was no such being. He had passed through the fire and had come out unscathed. His troubles had ennobled him. He showed himself to be a gentle, affectionate and lovable creature, as amiable as a happy woman, free from any trace of cynicism or resentment, without a grievance and without an unkind word for anyone. I have never heard him complain. I have never heard him deplore his ruined life or resent the treatment he had received at the hands of callous keepers. His journey through life had been indeed along a *via dolorosa*, the road had been uphill all the way, and now, when the night was at its blackest and the way most steep, he had suddenly found himself, as it were, in a friendly inn, bright with light and warm with welcome. His gratitude to those about him was pathetic in its sincerity and eloquent in the childlike simplicity with which it was expressed.

As I learned more of this primitive creature I found that there were two anxieties which were prominent in his mind and which he revealed to me with diffidence. He was in the occupation of the rooms assigned to him and had been assured that he would be cared for to the end of his days. This, however, he found hard to realize, for he often asked me timidly to what place he would next be moved. To understand his attitude it is necessary to remember that he had been moving on and moving on all his life. He knew no other state of existence. To him it was normal. He had passed from the workhouse to the hospital, from the hospital back to the workhouse, then from this town to that town or from one showman's caravan to another. He had never known a home nor any semblance of one. He had no possessions. His sole belongings, besides his clothes and some books, were the monstrous cap and the cloak. He was a wanderer, a pariah and an outcast. That his quarters at the hospital were his for life he could not understand. He could not rid his mind of the anxiety which had pursued him for so many years—where am I to be taken next?

Another trouble was his dread of his fellow-men, his fear of people's eyes, the dread of being always stared at, the lash of the cruel mutterings of the crowd. In his home in Bedstead Square he was secluded; but now and then a thoughtless porter or a wardmaid would open his door to let curious friends have a peep at the Elephant Man. It therefore seemed to him as if the gaze of the world followed him still.

Influenced by these two obsessions he became, during his first few weeks at the hospital, curiously uneasy. At last, with much hesitation, he said to me one day: "When I am next moved can I go to a blind asylum or to a lighthouse?" He had read about blind asylums in the newspapers and was attracted by the thought of being among people who could not see. The lighthouse had another charm. It meant seclusion from the curious. There at least no one could open a door and peep in at him. There he would forget that he had once been the Elephant Man. There he would escape the vampire showman. He had never seen a lighthouse, but he had come upon a picture of the Eddystone, and it appeared to him that this lonely column of stone in the waste of the sea was such a home as he had longed for.

I had no great difficulty in ridding Merrick's mind of these ideas. I wanted him to get accustomed to his fellow-men, to become a human being himself and to be admitted to the communion of his kind. He appeared day by day less frightened, less haunted looking, less anxious to hide, less alarmed when he saw his door being opened. He got to know most of the people about the place, to be accustomed to their comings and goings, and to realize that they took no more than a friendly notice of him. He could only go out after dark, and on fine nights ventured to take a walk in Bedstead Square clad in his black cloak and his cap. His greatest adventure was on one moonless evening when he walked alone as far as the hospital garden and back again.

To secure Merrick's recovery and to bring him, as it were, to life once more, it was necessary that he should make the acquaintance of men and women who would treat him as a normal and intelligent young man and not as a monster of deformity. Women I felt to be more important than men in bringing about his transformation. Women were the more frightened of him, the more disgusted at his appearance and the more apt to give way to irrepressible expressions of aversion when they came into his presence. Moreover, Merrick had an admiration of women of such a kind that it attained almost to adoration. This was not the outcome of his personal experience. They were not real women but the products of his imagination. Among them was the beautiful mother surrounded, at a respectful distance, by heroines from the many romances he had read.

His first entry to the hospital was attended by a regrettable incident. He had been placed on the bed in the little attic, and a nurse had been instructed to bring him some food. Unfortunately she had not been fully informed of Merrick's unusual appearance. As she entered the room she saw on the bed, propped up by white pillows, a monstrous figure as hideous as an Indian idol. She at once dropped the tray she was carrying and fled, with a shriek, through the door. Merrick was too weak to notice much, but the experience, I am afraid, was not new to him.

He was looked after by volunteer nurses whose ministrations were somewhat formal and constrained. Merrick, no doubt, was conscious that their service was purely official, that they were merely doing what they were told to do and that they were acting rather as automata than as women. They did not help him to feel that he was of their kind. On the contrary, they, without knowing it, made him aware that the gulf of separation was immeasurable.

Feeling this, I asked a friend of mine, a young and pretty widow, if she thought she could enter Merrick's room with a smile, wish him good morning and shake him by the hand. She said she could and she did. The effect upon poor Merrick was not quite what I had expected. As he let go her hand he bent his head on his knees and sobbed until I thought he would never cease. The interview was over. He told me afterwards that this was the first woman who had ever smiled at him, and the first woman, in the whole of his life, who had shaken hands with him. From this day the transformation of Merrick commenced and he began to change, little by little, from a hunted thing into a man. It was a wonderful change to witness and one that never ceased to fascinate me.

Merrick's case attracted much attention in the papers, with the result that he had a constant succession of visitors. Everybody wanted to see him. He must have been visited by almost every lady of note in the social world. They were all good enough to welcome him with a smile and to shake hands with him. The Merrick whom I had found shivering behind a rag of a curtain in an empty shop was now conversant with duchesses and countesses and other ladies of high degree. They brought him presents, made his room bright with ornaments and pictures, and, what pleased him more than all, supplied him with books. He soon had a large library and most of his day was spent in reading. He was not the least spoiled; not the least puffed up; he never asked for anything; never presumed upon the kindness meted out to him, and was always humbly and profoundly grateful. Above all he lost his shyness. He liked to see his door pushed open and people to look in. He became acquainted with most of the frequenters of Bedstead Square, would chat with them at his window and show them some of his choicest presents. He improved in his speech, although to the end his utterances were not easy for strangers to understand. He was beginning, moreover, to be less conscious of his unsightliness, a little disposed to think it was after all, not so very extreme. Possibly this was aided by the circumstance that I would not allow a mirror of any kind in his room.

The height of his social development was reached on an eventful day when Queen Alexandra—then Princess of Wales—came to the hospital to pay him a special visit. With that kindness which marked every act of her life, the Queen entered Merrick's room smiling and shook him warmly by the hand. Merrick was transported with delight. This was beyond even his most extravagant dream. The Queen made many people happy, but I think no gracious act of hers ever caused such happiness as she brought into Merrick's room when she sat by his chair and talked to him as to a person she was glad to see.

Merrick, I may say, was now one of the most contented creatures I have chanced to meet. More than once he said to me: "I am happy every hour of the day." This was good to think upon when I recalled the half-dead heap of miserable humanity I had seen in the corner of the waiting-room at Liverpool Street. Most men of Merrick's age would have expressed their joy and sense of contentment by singing or whistling when they were alone. Unfortunately poor Merrick's mouth was so deformed that he could neither whistle nor sing. He was satisfied to express himself by beating time upon the pillow to some tune that was ringing in his head. I have many times found him so occupied when I have entered his room unexpectedly. One thing that always struck me as sad about Merrick was the fact that he could not smile. Whatever his delight might be, his face remained expressionless. He could weep but he could not smile.

The Queen paid Merrick many visits and sent him every year a Christmas card with a message in her own handwriting. On one occasion she sent him a signed photograph of herself. Merrick, quite overcome, regarded it as a sacred object and would hardly allow me to touch it. He cried over it, and after it was framed had it put up in his room as a kind of ikon. I told him that he must write to Her Royal Highness to thank her for her goodness. This he was pleased to do, as he was very fond of writing

letters, never before in his life having had anyone to write
to. I allowed the letter to be dispatched unedited. It began
"My dear Princess" and ended "Yours very sincerely."
Unorthodox as it was it was expressed in terms any court-
ier would have envied.

Other ladies followed the Queen's gracious example and
sent their photographs to this delighted creature who had
been all his life despised and rejected of men. His
mantelpiece and table became so covered with photographs of handsome ladies, with dainty knickknacks and
pretty trifles that they may almost have befitted the
apartment of an Adonis-like actor or of a famous tenor.

Through all these bewildering incidents and through the
glamour of this great change Merrick still remained in
many ways a mere child. He had all the invention of an
imaginative boy or girl, the same love of "make-believe,"
the same instinct of "dressing up" and of personating
heroic and impressive characters. This attitude of mind was
illustrated by the following incident. Benevolent visitors
had given me, from time to time, sums of money to be
expended for the comfort of the *ci-devant* Elephant Man.
When one Christmas was approaching I asked Merrick what
he would like me to purchase as a Christmas present. He
rather startled me by saying shyly that he would like a
dressing-bag with silver fittings. He had seen a picture of
such an article in an advertisement which he had furtively
preserved.

The association of a silver-fitted dressing-bag with the
poor wretch wrapped up in a dirty blanket in an empty
shop was hard to comprehend. I fathomed the mystery in
time, for Merrick made little secret of the fancies that
haunted his boyish brain. Just as a small girl with a tinsel
coronet and a window curtain for a train will realize the
conception of a countess on her way to court, so Merrick

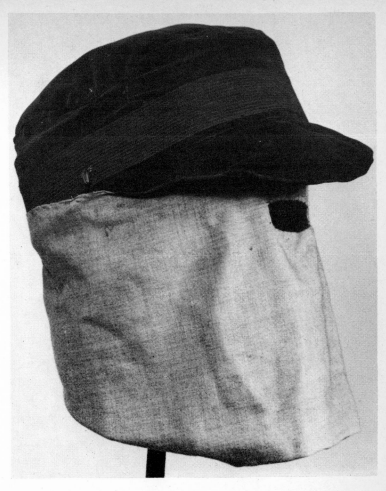

Figure 5, Cap and Mask Worn by Merrick on Excursions Outside His Rooms.

Figure 6, John Merrick's Imaginative Model of St Philip's Church.

loved to imagine himself a dandy and a young man about town. Mentally, no doubt, he had frequently "dressed up" for the part. He could "make-believe" with great effect, but he wanted something to render his fancied character more realistic. Hence the jaunty bag which was to assume the function of the toy coronet and the window curtain that could transform a mite with a pigtail into a countess.

As a theatrical "property" the dressing-bag was ingenious, since there was little else to give substance to the transformation. Merrick could not wear the silk hat of the dandy nor, indeed, any kind of hat. He could not adapt his body to the trimly cut coat. His deformity was such that he could wear neither collar nor tie, while in association with his bulbous feet the young blood's patent leather shoe was unthinkable. What was there left to make up the character? A lady had given him a ring to wear on his undeformed hand, and a noble lord had presented him with a very stylish walking-stick. But these things, helpful as they were, were hardly sufficing.

The dressing-bag, however, was distinctive, was explanatory and entirely characteristic. So the bag was obtained and Merrick the Elephant Man became, in the seclusion of his chamber, the Piccadilly exquisite, the young spark, the gallant, the "nut." When I purchased the article I realized that as Merrick could never travel he could hardly want a dressing-bag. He could not use the silver-backed brushes and the comb because he had no hair to brush. The ivory-handled razors were useless because he could not shave. The deformity of his mouth rendered an ordinary toothbrush of no avail, and as his monstrous lips could not hold a cigarette the cigarette-case was a mockery. The silver shoe-horn would be of no service in the putting on of his ungainly slippers, while the hat-brush was quite unsuited to the peaked cap with its visor.

Still the bag was an emblem of the real swell and of the
knockabout Don Juan of whom he had read. So every day
Merrick laid out upon his table, with proud precision, the
silver brushes, the razors, the shoe-horn and the silver
cigarette-case which I had taken care to fill with cigarettes.
The contemplation of these gave him great pleasure, and
such is the power of self-deception that they convinced
him he was the "real thing."

I think there was just one shadow in Merrick's life. As I
have already said, he had a lively imagination; he was
romantic; he cherished an emotional regard for women and
his favorite pursuit was the reading of love stories. He fell
in love—in a humble and devotional way—with, I think,
every attractive lady he saw. He, no doubt pictured himself
the hero of many a passionate incident. His bodily
deformity had left unmarred the instincts and feelings of
his years. He was amorous. He would like to have been a
lover, to have walked with the beloved object in the
langorous shades of some beautiful garden and to have
poured into her ear all the glowing utterances that he had
rehearsed in his heart. And yet—the pity of it!—imagine
the feelings of such a youth when he saw nothing but a
look of horror creep over the face of every girl whose eyes
met his. I fancy when he talked of life among the blind
there was a half-formed idea in his mind that he might be
able to win the affection of a woman if only she were
without eyes to see.

As Merrick developed he began to display certain modest
ambitions in the direction of improving his mind and
enlarging his knowledge of the world. He was as curious as
a child and as eager to learn. There were so many things he
wanted to know and to see. In the first place he was
anxious to view the interior of what he called "a real
house," such a house as figured in many of the tales he

knew, a house with a hall, a drawing-room where guests
were received and a dining-room with plates on the
sideboard and with easy chairs into which the hero could
"fling himself." The workhouse, the common lodging-
house and a variety of mean garrets were all the residences
he knew. To satisfy this wish I drove him up to my small
house in Wimpole Street. He was absurdly interested, and
examined everything in detail and with untiring curiosity. I
could not show him the pampered menials and the
powdered footmen of whom he had read, nor could I
produce the white marble staircase of the mansion of
romance nor the gilded mirrors and the brocaded divans
which belong to that style of residence. I explained that
the house was a modest dwelling of the Jane Austen type,
and as he had read *Emma* he was content.

A more burning ambition of his was to go to the theatre.
It was a project very difficult to satisfy. A popular
pantomime was then in progress at Drury Lane Theatre,
but the problem was how so conspicuous a being as the
Elephant Man could be got there, and how he was to see
the performance without attracting the notice of the
audience and causing a panic or, at least, an unpleasant
diversion. The whole matter was most ingeniously carried
through by that kindest of women and most able of
actresses—Mrs. Kendal. She made the necessary arrangements with the lessee of the theatre. A box was obtained.
Merrick was brought up in a carriage with drawn blinds
and was allowed to make use of the royal entrance so as to
reach the box by a private stair. I had begged three of the
hospital sisters to don evening dress and to sit in the front
row in order to "dress" the box, on the one hand, and to
form a screen for Merrick on the other. Merrick and I
occupied the back of the box which was kept in shadow.
All went well, and no one saw a figure, more monstrous

than any on the stage, mount the staircase or cross the corridor.

One has often witnessed the unconstrained delight of a child at its first pantomime, but Merrick's rapture was much more intense as well as much more solemn. Here was a being with the brain of a man, the fancies of a youth and the imagination of a child. His attitude was not so much that of delight as of wonder and amazement. He was awed. He was enthralled. The spectacle left him speechless, so that if he were spoken to he took no heed. He often seemed to be panting for breath. I could not help comparing him with a man of his own age in the stalls. This satiated individual was bored to distraction, would look wearily at the stage from time to time and then yawn as if he had not slept for nights; while at the same time Merrick was thrilled by a vision that was almost beyond his comprehension. Merrick talked of this pantomime for weeks and weeks. To him, as to a child with the faculty of make-believe, everything was real; the palace was the home of kings, the princess was of royal blood, the fairies were as undoubted as the children in the street, while the dishes at the banquet were of unquestionable gold. He did not like to discuss it as a play but rather as a vision of some actual world. When this mood possessed him he would say: "I wonder what the prince did after we left?" or "Do you think that poor man is still in the dungeon?" and so on and so on.

The splendor and display impressed him, but, I think, the ladies of the ballet took a still greater hold upon his fancy. He did not like the ogres and the giants, while the funny men impressed him as irreverent. Having no experience as a boy of romping and ragging, of practical jokes or of "larks," he had little sympathy with the doings of the clown, but, I think (moved by some mischievous instinct in his subconscious mind), he was pleased when the policeman was smacked in the face, knocked down and generally rendered undignified.

Later on another longing stirred the depths of Merrick's mind. It was a desire to see the country, a desire to live in some green secluded spot and there learn something about flowers and the ways of animals and birds. The country as viewed from a wagon on a dusty high road was all the country he knew. He had never wandered among the fields nor followed the windings of a wood. He had never climbed to the brow of a breezy down. He had never gathered flowers in a meadow. Since so much of his reading dealt with country life he was possessed by the wish to see the wonders of that life himself.

This involved a difficulty greater than that presented by a visit to the theatre. The project was, however, made possible on this occasion also by the kindness and generosity of a lady—Lady Knightley—who offered Merrick a holiday home in a cottage on her estate. Merrick was conveyed to the railway station in the usual way, but as he could hardly venture to appear on the platform the railway authorities were good enough to run a second-class carriage into a distant siding. To this point Merrick was driven and was placed in the carriage unobserved. The carriage, with the curtains drawn, was then attached to the mainline train.

He duly arrived at the cottage, but the housewife (like the nurse at the hospital) had not been made clearly aware of the unfortunate man's appearance. Thus it happened that when Merrick presented himself, his hostess, throwing her apron over her head, fled, gasping, to the fields. She affirmed that such a guest was beyond her powers of endurance for, when she saw him, she was "that took" as to be in danger of being permanently "all of a tremble."

Merrick was then conveyed to a gamekeeper's cottage which was hidden from view and was close to the margin of a wood. The man and his wife were able to tolerate his presence. They treated him with the greatest kindness, and with them he spent the one supreme holiday of his life. He could roam where he pleased. He met no one on his wanderings, for the wood was preserved and denied to all but the gamekeeper and the forester.

There is no doubt that Merrick passed in this retreat the happiest time he had as yet experienced. He was alone in a land of wonders. The breath of the country passed over him like a healing wind. Into the silence of the wood the fearsome voice of the showman could never penetrate. No cruel eyes could peep at him through the friendly undergrowth. It seemed as if in this place of peace all stain had been wiped away from his sullied past. The Merrick who had once crouched terrified in the filthy shadows of a Mile End shop was now sitting in the sun, in a clearing among the trees, arranging a bunch of violets he had gathered.

His letters to me were the letters of a delighted and enthusiastic child. He gave an account of his trivial adventures, of the amazing things he had seen, and of the beautiful sounds he had heard. He had met with strange birds, had startled a hare from her form, had made friends with a fierce dog, and had watched the trout darting in a stream. He sent me some of the wild flowers he had picked. They were of the commonest and most familiar kind, but they were evidently regarded by him as rare and precious specimens.

He came back to London, to his quarters in Bedstead Square, much improved in health, pleased to be "home" again and to be once more among his books, his treasures and his many friends.

Some six months after Merrick's return from the country he was found dead in bed. This was in April 1890. He was lying on his back as if asleep, and had evidently died suddenly and without a struggle, since not even the coverlet of the bed was disturbed. The method of his death was peculiar. So large and so heavy was his head that he could not sleep lying down. When he assumed the recumbent position the massive skull was inclined to drop backwards, with the result that he experienced no little distress. The attitude he was compelled to assume when he slept was very strange. He sat up in bed with his back supported by pillows; his knees were drawn up, and his arms clasped round his legs, while his head rested on the points of his bent knees.

He often said to me that he wished he could lie down to sleep "like other people." I think on this last night he must, with some determination, have made the experiment. The pillow was soft, and the head, when placed on it, must have fallen backwards and caused a dislocation of the neck. Thus it came about that his death was due to the desire that had dominated his life—the pathetic but hopeless desire to be "like other people."

As a specimen of humanity, Merrick was ignoble and repulsive; but the spirit of Merrick, if it could be seen in the form of the living, would assume the figure of an upstanding and heroic man, smooth browed and clean of limb, and with eyes that flashed undaunted courage.

His tortured journey had come to an end. All the way he, like another, had borne on his back a burden almost too grievous to bear. He had been plunged into the Slough of Despond, but with manly steps had gained the farther shore. He had been made "a spectacle to all men" in the heartless streets of Vanity Fair. He had been ill-treated and reviled and bespattered with the mud of Disdain. He had escaped the clutches of the Giant Despair, and at last had reached the "Place of Deliverance," where "his burden loosed from off his shoulders and fell from off his back, so that he saw it no more."

Chapter 3

Personality Development, Human Nature And Experience

Of all man's inborn dispositions there is none more heroic than the love in him. Everything else accepts defeat and dies, but love will fight no-love every inch of the way.

Laurens van der Post, *Flamingo Feather*

Background Of "The Elephant Man"

From an obituary notice in the *British Medical Journal* for 19 April 1890 we learn that "according to his relatives" John Merrick had reached the age of twenty-seven years at

39

the time of his death. The obituarist goes on to add, "It is almost certain that he was born with enlargement of the bones of the skull, right arm, and feet. When a child his skin was simply thickened, loose, and rough. He suffered in youth from disease of the hip-joint, which caused permanent lameness."*

The first part of this statement suggest that the information about Merrick's youth was supplied by the abovementioned "relatives." At least one of them, a paternal uncle, a hairdresser, attended his nephew's inquest.** How Merrick came to engage in the business of exhibiting himself there is no mention and we can only conjecture. Nor do we have any real clues as to the age at which he was sent to the workhouse.

As for information from Merrick himself, the past for him had been a nightmare, and as Treves tells us, it was too painful for him to talk about. Hence, Treves could learn little of it from Merrick. Of his father, according to Treves, Merrick knew absolutely nothing. But something does not quite fit here. We know from the report of Merrick's death in the London *Times* that his father was an engine-driver, who was alive and well at the time of the death.† Merrick must, at least, have heard about him from his other relatives. That he may not have remembered him, and chose not to speak of him, suggests that the father abandoned wife and child soon after Merrick was born.

It is to be gathered from Treves' account that Merrick

---

*See Appendix 8.

**See Appendix 7.

†See Appendix 7.

knew not much more of his mother than he did of his father. "In his subconscious mind," writes Treves, "there was apparently a germ of recollection in which someone figured who had been kind to him. He clung to this conception and made it more real by invention, for since the day since he could toddle no one had been kind to him." He believed firmly that his mother was very beautiful. It is quite possible that she was. But that is not the point. Treves suspects that Merrick had no recollection of his mother at all. But again Treves' comments here do not seem to be quite in accord with the facts. From Mr. Carr Gomm's letter, written on 30 November 1886 and published in the *Times* on December 4, we learn that Merrick carried a small painting of his mother with him.* That portrait, which could not have been much larger than a sizable miniature, was his most precious possession.** It represented more than "a germ of recollection": to him—it *was* his mother. (That the portrait of his mother was a painting is to be explained by the fact that during the Victorian period, especially during its first half, painting, ranging all the way from miniature to full-length canvas, rather than photography, was the customary means of making a permanent record of someone's appearance.) Writing more than thirty years after the events he was

----

*In all his references to "the Elephant Man" Treves gives his name as John Merrick. Mr. Carr Gomm, in his two letters to the editor of the *Times*, written over a four-year interval, 30 November 1886 and 15 April 1890, refers to him as "Joseph Merrick." In the report of the inquest on Merrick, published in the *Times* 16 April 1890, he is also referred to as "Joseph Merrick." But in all other references to him the name is given as John Merrick. What, in fact, was Merrick's actual given name?

**See Appendix 4.

recalling, Treves, who would undoubtedly have known of
the existence of this portrait, may simply have forgotten
about it. There remains still another possibility concerning
Merrick's knowledge of his mother: it may well be that she
visited him while he was in the workhouse, and that his
recollection of her was based on those visits. The fact that
at Merrick's inquest his father was mentioned as being alive
and well, and that no mention at all was made of his
mother suggests that she died young, considerably before
Merrick's death.*   .

Yet it is strange that nowhere does Treves make mention
of the painting. Treves must surely have seen it. That he
completely forgot about it may well mean that he had
already made up his mind about Merrick's mother, and
that Merrick's attachment to the painting was incompat-
ible with the particular theory he chose to embrace
concerning her. The nineteenth century was not kind in its
judgments of women, and it was easy to fall into a
pejorative view of a woman who could have placed so
helpless a creature in the workhouse.

Treves speaks harshly of Merrick's mother as "worthless and inhuman," for, he says, she abandoned her
deformed infant to the workhouse. But who can tell to
what agonies and pressures the poor woman had been
subjected? The burden of caring for a child so deformed,
the constant reminder and presence of so terrible an
affliction, the unremitting emotional stress, can only be
imagined by those who have had the misfortune to live

---

*See Appendix 7.

with a seriously deformed or disordered child. Present-day studies reveal that such an experience can be seriously disturbing to every member and disruptive of the whole family.[5] It is usually better for the family that such a child be sent to an institution. We may, in charity, believe that it was more likely that the decision to send little John Merrick to the workhouse was for his mother the only thing she could do—not because she was worthless and inhuman, but because she could no longer endure the suffering that his presence insured, and we may presume, also, the pressures that were brought to bear upon her. So it was probably sometime in 1866 or 1867, when the child was no more than three or four years old, that the pathetic creature was sent to the workhouse in Leicester.

Merrick came from a working-class family. The fact that at the time of his death his father was employed as an engine-driver, and his paternal uncle employed as a hairdresser, indicates that they were "respectable" working-class people and far from destitute. The presumption is that the father abandoned both his wife and his deformed son soon after Merrick's birth, leaving the mother to shift for herself. I have the feeling that she married somewhat beneath her station. What became of her is unknown. The evidence, as we have seen, indicates that she died not more than a few years after Merrick entered the workhouse.

Two statements that may have a bearing upon the age at which Merrick was entered at the workhouse are first, Treves' observation in his 1885 report of Merrick's case presented before the Pathological Society of London that "there was no evidence of similar deformities in any of his relatives," and second, his report there that Merrick "gave an elaborate story of a fright his mother had received shortly before his birth from having been knocked down by an elephant in a circus."* Both these statements could be taken to suggest that Merrick was older than three or four years when he entered the workhouse. A little deduction shows us this. Thus, on the assumption that Treves had not been in touch with any of Merrick's relatives, he would have had to obtain his information relating to their freedom from any such disorder from Merrick himself, and if Merrick depended upon memory for these recollections, then he must have been older than three or four years when he entered the workhouse. It is, however, quite likely that he was, from time to time, visited by relatives, and that he obtained such information as he had from them. The same holds true for the circus story. He may have heard this from his mother or later from his visiting relatives. The fact that Merrick claimed to recall his mother as being very beautiful may, despite Treves' dismissal of it as joyful "fiction," have been based on an actual memory of her, in which case Merrick must have been older than three years. In any event, there was the portrait of her which he had always with him. We shall probably not be far wrong in concluding that he was between three and four years of age—he may have been older—when he was taken to the workhouse.**

---

*See Appendix 3.

**In his report of Merrick's disorder made to the Pathological Society of London, 17 March 1885 (see Appendix 2), Treves states that Merrick was at the time aged twenty-four, and that he "earned a living by exhibiting himself as 'the Elephant Man.' " The age given by Treves would correspond with the age recorded at his death, as reported in the London *Times* (see Appendix 7).

In reconstructing Merrick's life, it appears that Merrick spent some ten or more years in the workhouse. As his disorder progressed he was shuttled from workhouse to hospital to workhouse and back again to hospital. It could hardly have been a more miserable existence. In the hospital, Treves surmised, he was taught to read and write, as well as other simple skills such as modelmaking, and the like. The Bible and the Prayer Book, which he knew intimately, were apparently the only books allowed him, and except for some scraps of newspaper, and an odd story picked up adventitiously, his education was minimal.

In early youth Merrick entered a hospital for treatment of disease of the left hip, a disease which left him permanently lame. The treatment had been long and painful, and from about the time of his discharge from hospital, sometime in his fourteenth year, he entered into an arrangement with a showman, who was but the first of a long series of "impresarios" who mercilessly exploited the defenseless youth.

Merrick's disease progressively worsened, so that he became increasingly an object calculated to produce horror and disgust in the crowds to which he was exhibited. This never-ending torment went on for some six years, in which

---

But there is reason to believe that Merrick was some two to three years younger. In 1886 it was stated that he "is about twenty-seven years of age" (see Appendix 5). In the report of his death in the *British Medical Journal* it is stated that he had "reached the age of 27, according to his relatives" (see Appendix 8). Since this report was almost certainly written by Treves, and based on a statement supplied by relatives, it would perhaps be most reasonable to assume that twenty-seven was nearer his actual age at the time of his death, which would have made him between twenty-one and twenty-two years of age at the time of his discovery by Treves.

each hour must have seemed like a day, and each day like a year, an eternal torture from which there could be no release.

In that charming novel *Memoirs of a Midget* by Walter de la Mare, the tiny heroine reflects upon her condition: "Again and again, as I have pored over the scenes of my memory, I have asked myself: What can life be about? What does it mean? What was my true course? Where my compass? How many times, too, have I vainly speculated what *inward* difference being a human creature of my dimensions really makes. What is—deep, deep in—at variance between Man and Midget?"[6] How many times must Merrick have asked himself the similar poignant questions. "Why me? Why this? What is the answer? Will there never be an end to this torment, this Gehenna?"

There was to be a release, at any rate, and it was to come in a wholly unexpected manner.

A recently vacated greengrocer's shop, opposite the London Hospital, the presence at the latter of a young surgeon and anatomist, who happened to be walking by when his eye caught the hastily improvised, gaudily painted announcement that "The Elephant Man" was to be seen within for an admission fee of twopence, and Treves' card, constituted the fortunate concatenation of events which, just two years later, in December 1866, was to free Merrick from his nightmare existence, and for the remaining three and a quarter years of his life, provide him with congenial surroundings and kind friends.

Having gained a view of "the Elephant Man," Treves, never before having seen such a case, strongly felt that the extraordinary "disease" should be described for the benefit of his colleagues. What better way to do this than to present before them the poor afflicted "Elephant Man" himself. Treves somehow, probably for a small consideration, persuaded both Merrick and his manager to allow him to be presented at a meeting of the Pathological Society of London at its rooms. Treves made all the arrangements and provided transportation to and from the Society's rooms. The meeting took place on the evening of Tuesday, 2 December 1884. It was at this time that the photographs shown in fig. 7 were made.* Some three months later, on Tuesday, 17 March 1885, Treves gave a more detailed account of "the Elephant Man" before the Pathological Society, this time illustrated with photographs. There was some discussion of the case by Dr. H. R. Crocker and Dr. Tilbury Fox. It was noted that changes in the bones had not been previously described in such cases.**

After the presentation at the Pathological Society Merrick returned in a cab to the shop in Whitechapel Road. But the next day it was empty, the police having forbidden the exhibition, and Merrick and his manager were gone. In order to admit him to the hospital, where he was to be photographed, Treves had given him his card. This was shortly after their first meeting. Exactly two years later this card was to prove the magic talisman to the last few happy years that Merrick was to spend.

As Treves writes:

> Those who are interested in the evolution of character might speculate as to the effect of this brutish life upon a sensitive and intelligent man. It would be reasonable to surmise that he would become a spiteful and malignant misanthrope, swollen with venom and filled with hatred of his fellow-men, or, on the other hand, that he would degenerate into a despairing melancholic on the verge of idiocy. Merrick, however, was no such being. He had

---

*See Appendix 1.

**See Appendix 2.

passed through the fire and had come out unscathed. His troubles had ennobled him. He showed himself to be a gentle, affectionate and lovable creature, as amiable as a happy woman, free from any trace of cynicism or resentment, without a grievance and without an unkind word for anyone. I have never heard him complain. I have never heard him deplore his ruined life or resent the treatment he had received at the hands of callous keepers. His journey through life had been indeed along a *via dolorosa,* the road had been uphill all the way, and now, when the night was at its blackest and the way most steep, he had suddenly found himself, as it were, in a friendly inn, bright with light and warm with welcome. His gratitude to those about him was pathetic in its sincerity and eloquent in the childlike simplicity with which it was expressed.

Treves clearly recognizes the fascinating problem that Merrick's personality presents, and he states it unequivocally: how could a creature so maltreated by Fate, so shockingly deformed and constantly wracked by pain, so brutally treated by his fellow men, have managed, in spite of everything, to emerge so unscarred, indeed, with so gentle, kind and magnanimous a personality?

It is to the consideration of these questions that we may now address ourselves.

Mothering And Personality

In the light of present-day psychological theory John Merrick constitutes an intriguing case history. There exists a great body of evidence, both observational and experimental, which indicates that maternal love or its equivalent is fundamentally important for the subsequent healthy development of the personality.[7] On the whole, this generalization appears to be sound. Exceptions are sometimes encountered.[8] It is such exceptions that are often most illuminating, not alone testing the generalization, but also often extending our understanding of the variability of the workings of human nature.

And what is human nature? Is human nature something with which we are born, or is it something we learn? The answer to that question is not simple, but however that may be, the best we can do is to say that human nature represents the expression of the interaction between our genetic potentials and the environmental challenges and pressures (we may consider consciousness part of the environment) to which those genetic potentials have been exposed.

Does the case of John Merrick, "the Elephant Man," constitute an exception to the rule that maternal love or its equivalent during the first half dozen years of life is fundamental to the development of mental health? And what is mental health? Without claiming too much, perhaps it is best described as that attribute or complex of attributes, so varyingly present in human beings, which is characterized by the ability to love, to work, and to play.

Merrick's pitiable suffering in unrelieved anguish from his ever-worsening physical deformities made his life a burden of pain. Added to this hardly supportable load of affliction was the constant humiliation and frustration to which he was subjected by his exploiters and the crowds to whom he was exhibited. That he should have emerged from these trials and tribulations so amiable and sensitive a character, greatly enlarges, I think, our understanding of the nature of human nature. The deformed experience of Merrick did not lead to the development of a deformed personality.

The Case Of Alexander Pope

Alexander Pope (1688-1744), one of the most gifted poets of all time, who from childhood was sickly, twisted, hunchbacked, dwarfed, aware during the greater part of his life that his deformities were the subject of laughter, ridicule, and sheer cruel malignity, responded somewhat differently to his lot, even though he enjoyed so many greater advantages, than John Merrick. No one could have been more sensitive to the ugliness of his misshapen body than Pope. He likened himself to a spider, a not inept description, for Pope lived in a sort of convoluted web of his own spinning in which it was his delight to entangle his victims, and pour over them his acidulous words so that they could escape not even from the passage of Time itself. The corrosive effect of his preoccupation with his deformities was evident to all who came in contact with him, it bit deep into his character, and by attrition gradually wore his integrity away. As J. H. Plumb has written:

All understanding of Pope must begin with his deformity, an ugly, terrible sight which he, as much as his friends, wished to ignore but could not. Like an ineradicable dye it stained all thought, all feeling. Deformity is commonly hideous in its effects. It corrodes character, leading to deceit, treachery, malignity and false living; and as often as not vitiates those entangled in the sufferer's life as much as the sufferer himself. So it was with Pope.[9]

But so it was not with John Merrick.

Pope all through his childhood and youth received a good deal of attention from his parents, and was greatly admired by his early teachers, for from the age of twelve he was entirely self-taught, a Catholic in a Protestant world. He was early recognized and esteemed as a prodigy. Throughout his childhood he enjoyed the comforts and encouragements of a comfortable middle-class home in the country. In fact, Pope remained a pampered child all the days of his life. In spite of detractors and enemies, the world of fashion, men and women of the highest station, the most distinguished writers of the day sought him out and lavished their praises upon him. Pope's writings had brought him considerable wealth. Yet he felt it necessary to pillory his detractors in such poems as *The Dunciad*, and by resort to such remarks, on which he worked like a lapidary, "The malice of my calumniators equals their stupidity. I forgive the first, pity the second, and despise both."

His words were brooded over and barbed, revealing the deep wounds that brought them forth. In spite of all the adulation, the slightest reference, intended or imagined, to his deformity would plunge Pope into an abyss of despair. From this he would emerge in frustration and rage plotting eternal damnation and destruction of the enemy. He never managed to come to terms with his deformity. He could not live with himself. Nor could he live with others. In *Eloisa and Abelard* he acknowledged his own tragic fate:

> Hearts so touch'd, so pierced, so lost as mine.
> E're such a soul regain its peaceful state,
> How often must it love, how often hate!
> How often hope, despair, resent, regret,
> Conceal, disdain—do all things but forget.

In his vanity, malevolence, lying, doubledealing, rage, and contempt for others, Pope was clearly reacting to the ineradicable and intolerable image of his bodily self which had become so damagingly fixed in his own mind. "There were few gestures in his life," writes Chard Powers Smith, "that were directed otherwise than to elevate himself or to debase a rival, and he was continually involved in one or more intrigues whose aim was to create the fictitious

public figure not only of Pope the great poet, but of Pope
the strong and courageous, the righteous and moral man.
Somebody—I think Swift—said that Pope could not drink
tea without a stratagem."[10]

How is it that with all the advantages of abiding parents,
admiring elders, a country home, considerable wealth, the
adulation of the fashionable and literary world, and above
all the consciousness of his genius, Pope should have
developed into so unpleasant a character, while poor,
terribly more hideously, deformed John Merrick, torn
from his mother at an early age, with the workhouse his
only home, followed by an unending course of the most
brutal and painful experiences, should have turned out to
be so amiable a personality?

Genes

One possible answer to the question of Merrick's
personality is the genetic one. It is conceivable that the
genes underlying that complex form of behavior which we
call "temperament" or "character" were largely responsible for the differences seen in the behavior of Pope and
Merrick. This is a possibility, but it is what Aristotle would
have called an improbable possibility. There can be little
question that genes play a role in influencing the development of temperament or character or personality, and that
whatever the experience with which those genes have
undergone interaction, they have played some part in
contributing to the structure of personality. That, however, is a very different thing from saying that the genes
have played the dominant or the largest role in deter-
mining personality.

In the first place, genes determine nothing. What genes

do is to *influence* the physiological development and expression of traits. The manner in which that influence will operate will depend to a great extent upon the interaction between those genes and the environments or experiences to which they have been exposed. Genes without environmental stimulation remain inert. Genetically identical plants when grown in the valleys look entirely different when they are grown near the timber line. Identical twins separated from one another at birth and brought up in different social and educational environments, may differ in both physical and intellectual growth in accordance with the differences in the environments in which they have been conditioned.[11] Yet genetically they remain identical. The power of the environment is very great, and differences in nutrition and education may make the most substantial kinds of differences in both physical and mental development.[12] As John Adams wrote to his wife Abigail, "Education has made a greater difference between man and man, than nature has been between man and brute."[13]

It is not, however, the difference in knowledge or in social competencies that concerns us here, but the difference in temperament, in personality. By temperament is meant the habitual frame of mind of the person. By personality is meant, in Gordon Allport's words, "the dynamic organization within the individual of those psychophysical systems that determine his unique adjustment to the environment."[14] It will be perceived that the terms "temperament" and "personality" have so much in common that they may be used interchangeably as having much, even if not exactly, the same meaning.

In short, it cannot be said that Merrick was temperamentally the man he was because of his genes. But the matter does not end here.

Heredity And Environment

Genes do not organize psychophysical systems, but environments, the social experience, the social stimulation to which the individual is exposed do tend strongly to organize the expression of the genetic potentials. The individual learns his adjustments to the environment for the most part, if not entirely, through the process of socialization, that is, the process whereby the individual acquires sensitivity to social stimuli, especially the pressures and obligations of group life, and learns to get along with, and behave like, others in his group or culture.

In the case of John Merrick it would seem reasonably clear that genes played a considerable role in equipping him with a genetic constitution (genotype) which disposed him to respond in the long-suffering, gentle, dignified manner in which he did—that is, adaptively, successfully—to the misfortunes that were so mercilessly aimed at him. It was, of course, not simply or even largely the effect of genes that was being expressed in his gentle personality. There can be no doubt that to some extent his personality was influenced by the early experiences which he had undergone, that there had been an interaction between those experiences and his genes. That must be taken as axiomatic; but it is not an unreasonable assumption, in the circumstances, that whatever the nature of his early socializing experiences, John Merrick's genetic constitution disposed him to make temperate low-keyed responses to the challenges with which he was confronted.

Again, it must be repeated that this is not to say that the genes involved determined that he would make a temperate response to the demands of the conditions to which he was exposed, but rather, if one may so put it, they tended to be strongly *influential* in that direction. The words are clumsy, and the matter so complex, it is difficult to be more precise in an area in which we actually know so little and understand even less. John Merrick's case does face us squarely with the heredity-environment problem. As customarily posed, this problem is an utterly spurious one, since it opposes and separates the unopposable and inseparable, falsely assuming heredity to be something that exists as an entity in itself altogether apart from environment. This is a fundamental error. Heredity is not an entity one inherits, but rather, heredity is the *expression* of something one inherits; it is *one's genetic constitution in interaction with the environment in which one's genes have developed.* The expression of that interaction between the genes and the environment constitutes one's heredity.[15]

Hence, John Merrick's heredity, like Pope's, and like every human being's who has ever lived, was comprised of both his genes and the environments in which those genes underwent development. By "environment" is meant anything lived, undergone or experienced—a highly various universe. Genes are no less various. They vary in their penetrance and expressivity. By *penetrance* is meant the regularity with which a gene produces its effect. When a gene regularly produces the same effect, it is said to have *complete penetrance*. When the trait is not manifested in some individuals, the gene is said to have *reduced penetrance*. By expressivity is meant the manifestation of a trait produced by a gene. When the manifestation differs from individual to individual, the gene is said to have *variable expressivity*, for example, the dominant gene for allergy may take such forms as asthma, eczema, hay fever, angioneurotic edema or urticarial rash.

We know so little about the genetics of behavior it is

difficult for us to say anything with certainty concerning the development of any genetical trait. It does not, however, seem unreasonable to suppose that the genes which are organized by the environment to participate in the structure of behavioral traits are characterized by much the same variability as the genes involved in the development of physical traits. Hence, it would be expected, other things being equal (which they seldom are), that genes for any behavioral trait would vary considerably in different individuals. No two individuals, not even so-called identical twins, have ever been alike in their genes or are ever likely to be. Considerable variability is the rule within the genetic constitution of every member of the human species. Both the expressivity and penetrance of "behavioral genes," as we may call them—that is, genes that are involved in the development and expression of behavior—will vary appreciably from individual to individual. It is because of this variability that, even if we were to conceive it possible and actually provide the impossible, an identical environment for every individual on this earth from birth to senility, we can be fairly certain that no two individuals would ever be anything but different in their behavioral traits as well as in some of their physical ones. Hence, we will be quite safe in attributing some of the behavioral differences between John Merrick and Alexander Pope to genetic factors. But that is about as far as it is possible for anyone to go in saying anything about the magnitude of the genetic contribution to the differences in their personalities.

That genes played some role in producing some of these differences is highly probable, but to what extent, it is impossible to say with any degree of security. At most it can be surmised that the genetic contribution was significant but not decisive.

Consciousness And Contrast

From what we know of Merrick's history it would seem evident that as soon as he came to be able to reflect upon his condition, unutterably miserable as he felt about it, he understood that there was no remedy for it, and that he would somehow have to live with it. And this Merrick seems to have resolved to do as best as he was able. To continue to live as a human being, in addition to continuing to drag so deformed and pain-wracked a body after him, constituted an ever-present challenge to him—not merely to survive, but to survive and live with dignity, no matter how strait the gate or charged with punishments the scroll. It must have been a conscious decision, in which, no doubt, the predisposing genes were a help, for without such a conscious decision Merrick would easily have fallen into the accidie and bitterness of an Alexander Pope. He accepted his physical deformities and the pain of his body as fate from which there was no escape. His role in life as an exhibition freak he also came to terms with, for he knew there was no escape from that either. But his mind, his soul, that he knew was in his own keeping, and with the limited resources that were at his disposal, no matter how mistreated by others, no matter what the menace of the years, he resolved to remain the master of that one holy kingdom left to him. There he could live in imagination as he would. In a way it was easier for him to live so than it was for Pope. Merrick knew that he had no more to expect from life than the lot to which he had been condemned—the possibility of any higher expectation, of relief from his disorder, of freedom to live as other men, was, he knew, beyond realization. To that irrevocable sentence he accommodated himself. But with Pope the case was far different.

The more successful Pope grew the more this fed his awareness of the contrast between what he was and what he might have been. That the greatest poet of his day should have been, in his own eyes, the meanest man of his time, a misshapen ugly dwarf, was a thought that grew, with the growth of his fame, like an intolerable excrescence upon his spirit. The thought never left him and oppressed him, his unsightliness making himself unsightly to himself—indeed, sicklied o'er with the pale cast of his thought—and exacerbated to the point where accepted by everyone he grew to be both unacceptable and unendurable to himself. Genes here, too, may have helped, but so, too, did the conditions of Pope's life.

Maternal Love

The case that loving maternal care is necessary for every child if it is to grow and develop as a mentally healthy human being has been developed by innumerable studies, the best known of which is John Bowlby's World Health Organization monograph, *Maternal Care and Mental Health,* published in 1951.* According to this view, as Bowlby puts it:

> . . . what is believed to be essential for mental health is that the infant and young child should experience a warm, intimate, and continuous relationship with his mother (or permanent mother-substitute) in which both find satisfaction and enjoyment. Given this relationship, the emotions of anxiety and guilt, which in excess characterize mental ill-health, will develop in a moderate and organized way. When this happens, the child's

---

*And also in a popular version entitled *Child Care and the Growth of Love*. Baltimore: Penguin Books, 1953.

characteristic and contradictory demands, on the one hand for unlimited love from his parents and on the other for revenge upon them when he feels that they do not love him enough, will likewise remain of moderate strength and become amenable to the control of his gradually developing personality. It is this complex, rich, and rewarding relationship with the mother in the early years, varied in countless ways by relations with the father and with siblings, that child psychiatrists and many others now believe to underlie the development of character and of mental health.

Bowlby goes on to add that direct studies "make it plain that, when deprived of maternal care, the child's development is almost always retarded—physically, intellectually, and socially—and that symptoms of physical and mental illness may appear . . . and that some children are gravely damaged for life."[16]

As this passage suggests and as I have noted, there are some exceptions to the pattern.[17] It has been pointed out that some children who have suffered maternal deprivation seem to have escaped severe lasting damage. This is true. There are unquestionably differences in vulnerability to maternal deprivation in different children. And, again, there may well be a genetic factor operating in such cases.

Furthermore, there are situations in which the relative absence of the mother does not harm the child. The kibbutz experience, for example, demonstrates that the constant presence of a loving mother is not essential for the development of mental health, as long as there are mother surrogates present who are able to give the child the loving care it requires. Moreover, in the communal nurseries of the kibbutz the child's parents visit it for two hours every day and usually they spend all day Saturday together, so that the child can scarcely be said to be deprived of its mother. What it enjoys is, if not altogether the best of all possible worlds, then something approximating thereto in a combination of institutional and maternal care. The results are said to be quite satisfactory by some,[18] not so satisfactory by others.[19]

Again, as Margaret Mead has pointed out, there is good evidence from comparative studies of various societies that it is possible to make children able to tolerate separation much more easily, because they trust more people.[20] One observes this in many nonliterate societies, especially those in which the extended family prevails—a loss from which urbanized societies suffer severely. The extended family, consisting of mother, father, their parents and siblings and their children, afforded the child much greater opportunities for varied human relationships and greater opportunities for the experience of affection than it enjoys in the contemporary atomized nuclear family.

Still, in the Western World it is the nuclear family unit, consisting of mother, father and children that is the prevailing institutional influence in the socialization of the child, and in this unit it is the mother who is most closely involved with the child from birth onwards. So that for most children in the Western World the mother has been the principal agent of socialization, the chief molder, of the child. It is one of the best substantiated hypotheses of modern behavioral science that in such families early experiences of deprivation will produce more or less serious and enduring personality disturbances.[21]

Critical Developmental Periods
And Merrick's Life

The evidence appears to be consistent with the developmental law that the earlier the deprivation of mother-love the greater is the damage done. Bowlby has drawn a parallel between the early development of the human mind and general embryological development. It is during the period extending from the fifth to the twelfth week of embryonic development that the organ systems develop. Clearly, any interference with the development of the organ-systems during that period will result in seriously disordering effects. So it is with the development of the human mind. For healthy behavioral growth and development it is necessary for the infant to be exposed to the organizing influences of a loving human being. Under normally healthy conditions, the person best designed to serve as the organizer, the humanizer, is the biological mother.

There is now much evidence which indicates that there are critical developmental periods in the life of every child during which it must receive certain kinds of stimulation if its potentialities for behavioral response are to develop. These critical developmental periods are as follows:

1. The period during which the infant is in process of establishing an explicit cooperative relationship with a clearly defined person—the mother; this is normally achieved by five or six months of age.

2. The period during which the child needs the mother as an ever-present support and companion; this normally continues to about the end of the third year.

3. The period during which the child is in process of becoming able to maintain a relationship with its mother during her absence. During the fourth and fifth years, under favorable conditions, such a relationship can be maintained for a few days or even a few weeks; after seven or eight years of age such a relationship can be maintained for longer periods, though not without some strain.

The process whereby the child simultaneously develops his own ego or self as well as his superego or system of incorporated parental standards, as well as his ability to maintain relationships with absent persons, is variously described as a process of identification, internalization, or introjection, since it is according to the models set by the parents that the functions of the ego and superego are incorporated within the total psyche.

We find that three somewhat different experiences can produce the lack-love or maternal deprivation syndrome, and so interrupt a child's normal process of development. These experiences are:

1. Lack of any opportunity to develop attachment to a mother-figure during the first three years.

2. Maternal deprivation for a period varying for days within the first and second years, and weeks or months during the third and fourth years.

3. Changes from one mother-figure to another during the first four or five years.

Unless the child has been firmly grounded in the discipline of love and interdependency, he is damaged in his ability to develop clear and definite judgments concerning people and things, and his ability to form such judgments as an adult is seriously handicapped. As adults the judgments of such persons tend to be blurred and vague. Their decisions about the world, people, and things tend to be characterized by doubt, suspicion, uncertainty, misgiving, and unsureness. They vacillate, in short, they tend to see the world through a mist of unshed tears. They are characterized by an inability to enter into the feelings of others because, when they were young, no one cared enough to enter into their feelings.

Many of the traits exhibited by Alexander Pope are characteristic of the individual who as a child was inadequately loved. While Pope's parents may have doted on him in his later childhood, it is quite probable that they did not give him all the attention he needed during his first three years. On the other hand, John Merrick's behavior strongly suggests that he had been much loved in his early years. Put another way, if mother-love in the early years of the child's development is as effective in securing the development of a healthy personality as theory and observation suggest, then it is very likely that John Merrick received a considerable amount of love from his mother during the first three or four years of his life. One can speculate on how this may have come about. At birth Merrick's deformities involved his head, his right arm, and his feet. Though slight then, in comparison to what they were later to become, the pitiable state of the child thus must have elicited more than an ordinary amount of loving care from his mother. As his disorder progressed it is quite likely that he received increasingly more maternal attention, until his mother was either persuaded or forced to send him to the workhouse.

We have one other item to support the view that Merrick received the love of his mother during his early years: the picture of her that he carried about with him. The letter that Mr. Carr Gomm wrote to the *Times* in November 1886 contains this moving and illuminating passage. "Through all the miserable vicissitudes of his life he had carried about a painting of his mother to show that she was a decent and presentable person, and as a memorial of the only one who was kind to him in life until he came under the kind care of the nursing staff of the London Hospital and the surgeon who had befriended him."*
This passage, I think, constitutes eloquent testimony to

---

*See Appendix 4.

the high probability that little John Merrick received a great deal of love from his mother. Unloved children do not carry portraits of their mothers about with them.

In any event, on any other assumption it would be difficult—although not impossible—to account for the strength, health, integrity and amiability of John Merrick's personality.

What other explanation might there be? As we have seen, it is a fact, and case histories have been reported by a number of investigators, that some children do manage to come through a lack-love infancy relatively unscathed. The possibility exists that John Merrick constitutes an example of such an exceptional case. In which event, he would, in common with those children whose early lack-love history is definitely known and who have emerged relatively undamaged, have to be accounted for, at least in part, on the basis of a genetic constitution that was exceptionally resistant to the privations of mothering that most children require for adequately healthy behavioral development.

As noted, the fact that Merrick's father was an engine-driver, and that the paternal uncle who appeared at Merrick's inquest in 1890 was a hairdresser tells us that Merrick came from a working-class family, a family that could have supported a normal child quite adequately. It must have been a hard decision to send the child to a workhouse, for no family in Victorian England would have sent anyone to the workhouse if it could possibly have been avoided. Even to the poor the very name "work-house" sounded like a knell, and justly conjured up images of the bleakest of all prisons, the last refuge of the abandoned and hopeless.

George Crabbe's description of the workhouse of the eighteenth century still held true for that of the nineteenth century.[22]

There children dwell who know no parents' care:
Parents, who know no Children's love, dwell there;
Heart-broken Matrons on their joyless bed,
Forsaken Wives and Mothers never wed;
Dejected Widows and unheeded tears,
And crippled Age with more than childhood's fears;
The Lame, the Blind, and, far the happiest they!
The moping Idiot and the Madman gay.

The fact that Merrick had no recollection of his father may mean that the latter had early abandoned his family or that Merrick was illegitimate, and that no father was about at all during his infancy. In either event this may well have worked to the advantage of the child, for without the presence of a husband Merrick's mother may have been able to devote most of her available time to her pathetically misshapen child. It was Merrick's father who appears to have been heartless, for he was aware of his son's plight and never, so far as we can discover, reached out a helping hand toward him, not even appearing at his inquest.* Merrick had neither brother nor sister.

Treves tells us that Merrick was a devoted reader, and that he was fond of writing letters. Where he had learned to read and write, whether in hospital or workhouse, we do not know. It may well have been in the workhouse to which he had been sent as a small child. We have already observed that he must have been in the workhouse for some ten years or more. We are told that he had the greatest horror of the workhouse, and justifiable as that may well have been Merrick was no doubt indebted for his ability to read and

---

*See Appendix 7.

write to his custodians in the workhouse. There is also some evidence that he there acquired one or two other skills, for Mr. Carr Gomm, chairman of the London Hospital, in his letter of 30 November 1886 to the editor of the *Times*, inviting contributions for the support of Merrick, in giving an account of his activities wrote that "He occupies his time in the hospital by making with his one available hand little cardboard models, which he sends to the matron, doctor, and those who have been kind to him."*

One such example of his handiwork has survived, and it speaks volumes for the acuity of his vision, his intelligence, his imagination, his manipulatory skill and his ability to make the most refined judgments as to distance and proportion.

From a window in his apartment at the London Hospital Merrick could see the Church of St. Philip at the corner of Oxford and Turner Streets, and also St. Augustine's, the hospital church that was being built at the time. Once comfortably settled into his new quarters and the routine of his new life Merrick embarked upon the ambitious task of making a model of a great church or cathedral. With the two churches as exemplars and the use of his imagination Merrick constructed from bits of carefully chosen pieces of colored paper and cardboard a beautifully impressive edifice (fig. 6). The model is preserved in a glass case in the London Hospital Medical College Museum. The photograph of the model shown in fig. 6 was shot through the glass case in which it was housed, in 1952. The details are perhaps not as sharp as they might otherwise have been, but from the photograph reproduced in fig. 6 some idea

---

*See Appendix 4.

may be gained of this remarkable achievement, all carried out with the use of one hand. Merrick's right hand, the reader may recall from Treves' account, was completely useless (see fig. 11). The model is really quite magnificent. Every stone, every tile, indeed, every detail the imaginative eye could possibly see in such a building is represented with singular fidelity in Merrick's model. It is in every way a quite astonishing performance, and all the more remarkable that the work was done with the use of the left hand only. When the need arose, Nurse Ireland, who looked after Merrick, probably helped him.

One cannot help wondering what Merrick might have achieved had Fate granted him a normal body and more favorable opportunities. Everyone who knew him remarked upon his high intelligence. Mr. Carr Gomm, in his 1886 letter to the *Times*, wrote, "Terrible though his appearance is, so terrible indeed that women and nervous persons fly in terror from the sight of him, and that he is debarred from seeking his livelihood in any ordinary way, yet he is superior in intelligence, can read and write, is quiet, gentle, not to say even refined in mind."*

Treves entertained the highest opinion of his intelligence. It is gratifying to reflect that at least in that function he was not, as by his disorder he might very easily have been, affected.

It is probable that Merrick acquired his skill in model-making during his sojourn in the workhouse. It may also have been that in spite of his expressed horror of it that some of his workhouse custodians may have shown him an occasional kindness, and helped him at critical moments to

---

*See Appendix 4.

retain a human relatedness. This is, of course, an assumption, but it is one not without some reason. That reason lies in the fact that a child who has been adequately loved during the first three or four years of his life, and who is then for the next several years unloved, is very likely to show some evidences of such unloving experience in his behavior. Such a child will often display a mixture of "good" and "bad" qualities. Having been adequately loved in his early years he will be capable of loving behavior, but having been unloved and frustrated in subsequent years, he may exhibit a certain amount of hostility, aggressiveness, opportunism, and selfishness. Merrick showed no such traits.

In his report of Merrick's disorder made to the Pathological Society of London, 17 March 1885 (see Appendix 2), Treves states that Merrick "earned a living by exhibiting himself as 'the Elephant Man,'" but this statement should not be taken to mean that Merrick did so on his own. It is very doubtful whether Merrick could ever have managed to exhibit himself without the aid of a manager or "impresario." Mr. Carr Gomm in his 1886 *Times* letter states that he and his manager "went halves in the net proceeds of his exhibition." And this appears to have been the arrangement into which Merrick entered with a series of "managers."

Treves writes of Merrick's dread of his fellow men, of his fear of being stared at, and his great desire for seclusion from the curious, even to the extent of being sent to a home for the blind, so that no one could see his deformed shape. "His sole idea of happiness," writes Treves, "was to creep into the dark and hide." This hardly suggests a person, however hard pressed, who would willingly have exposed himself to the humiliations heaped upon him by men, women and children who would gape at him with horror and revulsion, as if he were some frightful monster. Nor is it conceivable that a creature as sensitive as Merrick, had he once tried such exposure to the crowd would willingly have continued in it. And yet hunger, which at first may have driven him to enter into such an arrangement, may have forced him to continue in the only way of life that was possible for him.

We do not know how Merrick came to fall into the hands of the vampire showmen who dragged him from town to town. He was a captive slave who, much as he wanted to run away, was prevented from doing so if by nothing else than by his lameness. As it was, he could only walk with the aid of a stick. He was in the position of a dog tied to a post, traded like an animal from one showman to another. Such money as he managed to save was no doubt augmented by the pennies and halfpennies thrown to him by pitying spectators. Even this, according to Carr Gomm, was eventually stolen from him by the last of his managers.

Had Merrick been able to escape from his keepers, how could he, in fact, have supported himself? How could he, whose articulation was so poor that he could hardly make himself understood, have made the necessary arrangements? It is not a simple matter to exhibit oneself. Where could he have gone? Who would have taken him in? The sight he presented, with his long black cloak and the hood over his head, would have been frightening enough to cause every door to be shut against this apparition. Because of his appearance, so the 1886 account in the *British Medical Journal* reports, a steamboat captain refused to take him as a passenger. Even the Royal Hospital for Incurables and the Home for Incurables in London declined to take him in when, in 1886, he was finally rescued by Treves. Such frustrations and humiliations were his daily fare. In some ways, then, he was better off being in the charge of a custodian, rather than have to attempt to shift for himself. Merrick almost certainly was aware of this, for the only alternatives before him were in this way to remain in the keeping of a manager or be altogether abandoned to his own helpless self. There was always the workhouse, but to this Merrick would never voluntarily have returned, even had he been in a position to escape from his captors.

There was no possible means by which Merrick could have supported himself in Victorian England. It was difficult enough for normal men of the working classes even to manage so much as to subsist, and large numbers of them failed to do so.[23] Merrick may at first have entered into some arrangement with a manager to be exhibited as "The Elephant Man" in return for a share of the profits and his bed and board. Once embarked upon this course, repellent as it must have been to him, he found himself unable to escape from it.

What saved Merrick for the few happy years he was finally to enjoy was the police banning of such indecent exhibitions of a pitiful human being. He then became no longer profitable, and so, writes Treves, "The impresario, having robbed him of his paltry savings, gave him a ticket to London, saw him into the train and no doubt in parting condemned him to perdition."

This may be the true history of what actually happened, but I find it difficult to understand why the "impresario" who had been profiting from the exhibition of Merrick would not have abandoned him altogether, especially after stealing his money. Why go to the trouble and expense of paying for his ticket to London, and seeing him into the train? Can it be that he was not altogether lacking in human feeling? Or is it possible that he was forced by the police to pay for the deportation of Merrick and required to see him safely placed on the train?

There is, in any case, another account of these events. This was given by Mr. Carr Gomm in his 1886 letter to the *Times*. In this communication we learn that "Merrick was persuaded to go over to Belgium, where he was taken in hand by an Austrian, who acted as his manager . . . . But the police, there too, kept moving him on." The manager, seeing that the exhibition was pretty nearly played out, decamped with nearly fifty pounds of Merrick's life-savings, "and left him alone and absolutely destitute in a foreign country." Knowing no language but his own, and hardly being able to make himself understood in it, Merrick nevertheless managed to pawn something, and in this manner was able to raise enough money to pay his passage back to London.* From every viewpoint this would seem to be a more likely account of what actually occurred.

A point of interest is that in his report to the Pathological Society of London in March 1885 Treves states that two years previously a connective tissue band had been surgically removed from Merrick's mouth.** The operation had been performed at the Leicester Infirmary. This would have been in 1883 when Merrick was twenty or twenty-one. Merrick was born at or in the vicinity of Leicester, in central England. Could it be that by 1883 he had not yet left Leicester and only after that date fell into his exhibition way of life? In that event his life as an

---

*See Appendix 4.

**See Appendix 3.

exhibition freak would have been of much lesser duration than Treves seemed to suppose. Or could it be—which seems more likely—that since the oral obstruction interfered with speech and mastication of his food and it was impressed upon him that the growth must be removed surgically, that he returned to the one place he knew well for the operation? Without being able to eat Merrick would soon have died and his usefulness to his manager would have been at an end. He may well, then, have been taken to Leicester by one such person, and following recovery from the operation, which was a fairly simple one, they together resumed the road.

Merrick's Simplicity

Treves writes of Merrick that in his outlook upon the world he was a child, "an elemental being, so primitive that he might have spent the twenty-three years of his life [up to the time he came to rest in the London Hospital] immured in a cave."

Merrick was undoubtedly limited in his horizons, and possibly "primitive" in the sense that he had not matured in many of the traits that a normally socialized man develops, but he was scarcely "an elemental being," for childlike as he may have been in many ways, he was no illiterate Caliban, no "freckled whelp," discovered by a putative civilizing Prospero.

That he was in some ways a simple person is attested by the fact that in order to account for his condition he either accepted from others or created for himself the story of a fright his mother had received shortly before his birth from having been knocked down by an elephant at a circus. It is by no means surprising that Merrick should have clung to this belief. He needed some explanation for his condition, if only for himself, and this was better than most. The belief in "maternal impressions" is a very widespread one to this day, and it is of great antiquity. Nor is it entirely irrational.[24] It is quite understandable that a deformity which defied the abilities of the best physicians to explain should, in Merrick's unsophisticated mind, have found so clear and convincing a resolution.

But this simplicity did not distinguish the whole of Merrick's character. His self-discipline and his skill at constructing his cardboard models, to name only two traits, show a being capable of more than "simplicity."

Merrick's Personality

Treves states that "since the day he could toddle no one had been kind to him." If this were true then Merrick would, indeed, constitute an outstanding example of the constitutional ability of some children to resist the damaging effects of a lack-love infancy. But by "toddle" Merrick probably meant from the day he could remember. This could scarcely have been earlier than three or four years. It, therefore, still remains a strong possibility that up to that time he may well have received an adequate amount of mothering. Indeed, the evidence, as I have suggested, seems to point very much in this direction: namely, that John Merrick as an infant received much love from his mother, and that it is highly unlikely that from birth onward he experienced nothing but an unbroken history of deprivation.

Treves was fully aware of the dramatic value of the story he had to tell, and I cannot help but feel that he may well have exaggerated somewhat when he said that Merrick had neither childhood nor boyhood, and that he never experienced pleasure. Certainly Merrick could never have enjoyed the kind of childhood and boyhood that normal children experience. Certainly, he must have suffered keenly from the awareness that he was not like others, a repellent creature. But he had been a child who must have received some kindness, and taken some pleasure, at least, in reading and in doing the things with his hands that he was so capable of doing.

Had Merrick suffered a life of as total deprivation as Treves suggests, his story would, in fact, be utterly mystifying, for his personality then would be wholly inexplicable.

From all that we know of the development of human character, Merrick's personality could not have been what it was had he suffered from a lack-love infancy and childhood. Either our theory and observation of human development are wrong or Merrick constitutes an extraordinary exception to the rule. On the contrary, his case appears to confirm the rule, for no one could possibly have borne the torment of his later years and emerged from them as Merrick did had he not been fortified by the early experience of adequate love.

Apart from his limited experience and knowledge, it is quite possible that Merrick may have had some unexpressed psychological impairments, but what these may have been, if any, we do not know. The truth seems to be that in most ways he achieved a kind of mental health that defies most human beings, the ability to love, to work, and to play. If Merrick had any hidden psychological impairments they failed to become visible.

Such impairments as Merrick did exhibit are readily and clearly explicable as the result of his unfortunate experiences with most human beings to whom he had been exposed during the greater part of his life. Treves refers to his curious uneasiness after being put in possession of his rooms at the London Hospital. Merrick found it difficult to believe that he had at long last come into a safe harbor. He thought he might be moved on again, following the pattern of so much of his life when he was moved from place to place, town to town. He was anxious, timid, frightened, haunted-looking and alarmed when his door was opened.

These are the perfectly understandable reactions which even the healthiest of human beings would develop after being subjected to years of maltreatment and debasement. Until he reached the safe haven of the London Hospital, he said that he had never before known what quiet and rest were. As soon as Merrick became convinced that he had, indeed, come safely to rest, that his future was secure, that he no longer had anything to fear, and what is more, that he was a human being whom other human beings valued and treated with respect, he lost all his defensive reactions, and without in the least ever becoming froward, aggressive or presumptuous, he became a changed man. That he could say to Treves, more than once, "I am happy every hour of the day," must have been a most rewarding experience for Treves, and at the same time testifies to the recovery of Merrick from the nightmare existence of his former life. One does not, of course, ever recover completely from the scars inflicted by such an existence, but one can recuperate sufficiently to function healthily even though some scar tissue remains. This is what Merrick so eminently achieved.

Merrick's Life At The London Hospital

One cannot, without being deeply moved, read Treves' account of the occasion when, having persuaded a pretty young widow to visit Merrick and shake hands with him, he was so overcome by the experience that he broke down and sobbed until Treves thought he would never cease. Apart from his mother, the young woman was the first of her sex who had ever smiled at him, the first woman, in the whole of his life who had ever shaken hands with him. It was from that day that the transformation in Merrick began to take place, and he began to feel like a normal human being. It was the first human contact he had established with a woman in that way in his life.

From that day on Merrick never failed for ladies of note in the social world to visit him, including the Princess of Wales (later Queen Alexandra), Lady Dorothy Neville and the famous actress Mrs. Kendal. It was Mrs. Kendal who made it possible for Merrick to see his first play, seated in the shadows of a private box, screened from view by a row of nurses seated in front dressed in evening clothes. In spite of the immense trouble involved, Mrs. Kendal enabled Merrick to see other plays, the enchantment of which for Merrick would have been sufficient reward for any actor. It was the brilliant and ever-kind Mrs. Kendal who, at her own expense, obtained the services of a teacher to instruct Merrick in the art of basketmaking, an art at which Merrick soon excelled. (Mrs. Kendal died in 1935 at the age of eighty-seven, covered with honors and fondly remembered by everyone.)

From time to time the Prince of Wales, later Edward VII, sent Merrick game, and many gifts came to him from other personages. For three years and four months, with an occasional visit to the theater, with six-week stays in the country during the summer, Merrick lived happily in his rooms, his "home" as he called it, in the London Hospital. Rising in the afternoon he took his walks every day regularly in Bedstead Square, within the grounds of the hospital, and occupied himself with reading, model-making, and basket-making. His health was good. He was happy. It would seem that he would now enjoy many happy years in comfort and security. But it was not to be. On the night of 10 April 1890 Merrick took his usual walk, after which he retired for the evening. The next day at 1:30 in the afternoon the wardmaid brought him his dinner, which he did not eat. He appeared to be perfectly well at that time. Two hours later he was found dead.

Apart from his deformities and the increasing weight of his head, which he experienced more and more difficulty in holding upright, Merrick was as I have said in relatively good health, although he is believed to have suffered from some undiagnosed cardiac condition as well as bronchitis. There was no reason to believe that he did not have at least some more years before him, though it was expected that he would die suddenly. The fact that he did not touch his dinner suggests that he may have died shortly after the wardmaid left his room. Mr. Ashe, the house-surgeon, who was called to the deceased at 3:30 that Friday afternoon, said at the inquest he believed that death was due to asphyxia, that the weight of the head, while Merrick was taking a natural sleep, overcame him and so suffocated him by causing pressure on the windpipe.*

As Treves explained, Merrick's customary mode of

---

*See Appendix 7.

sleeping, owing to the great weight of his head, was in a seated position with his arms clasped round his legs and his head resting on his knees. His oft-expressed wish to Treves that he might lie down to sleep "like other people," may have, on this final occasion, as Treves suggests, impelled him to try the experiment, with consequences that were fatal. What probably happened is that his neck was dislocated, that the first neck vertebra (the atlas), as a consequence of the heavy head falling backward, slipped over the small finger-like process (the odontoid process) of the second neck vertebra, which, together with a ligament, normally keeps the first neck vertebra in place, and either ruptured or fatally compressed the spinal cord. I think it unlikely that asphyxia, as stated at the coroner's inquest, was the cause of death. Not even the coverlet of the bed was disturbed. There were no signs of a struggle for breath. With rupture or compression of the cord at that level of the neck death would have been instantaneous.

It would seem that the Fates had prearranged Merrick's life course and allotted him a brief span of years. Saddled with a deformed body and a hideous appearance, crippled, lame, tortured and tormented, the compassionate interest of a young surgeon and a public subscription enabled him to spend the last few years of his life in a happiness that was all the more intensely felt by contrast with the squalor and misery of his former existence.

Merrick bore with courage and dignity the hideous deformities and other ills with which he was afflicted. The nightmare existence he had led during the greater part of his life he put behind him. He never complained or spoke unkindly of those who had maltreated him. His suffering, like a cleansing fire, seems to have brought him nearer to that human condition in which all the nonessentials of life having fallen away, only the essential goodness of man remained. I cannot hope to improve upon Treves' final description of him. "As a specimen of humanity, Merrick was ignoble and repulsive; but the spirit of Merrick, if it could be seen in the form of the living, would assume the figure of an upstanding and heroic man, smooth browed and clean of limb, with eyes that flashed undaunted courage."

Chapter 4

The Nature Of
"The Elephant Man's"
Disorder

*Of themselves diseases come upon men
continually by day and by night,
bringing mischief to mortals silently.*

Hesiod, *Works and Days*

What was the nature of the condition from which John
Merrick suffered? What was it that so disordered his bones,
especially his skull and skin, as to make him one of the
most unfortunate of human beings? His skeleto-cutaneous
affliction caused him, among other things, to develop a
head so deformed that it was said to resemble an
elephant's. This was something of an exaggeration. The

resemblance was exceedingly remote, and yet, it was there. For the purpose of attracting the attention of those who would be willing to pay their pennies to gape at a man who looked like an elephant, "the Elephant Man" was as good a description as any. And so John Merrick became "the Elephant Man." The name was a showman's choice, and in no way bears any relation to the disease known as elephantiasis.

Elephantiasis is a disease due to infection by a threadlike worm *(Wucheri malayi)* which is transmitted by mosquitoes. Multiplication of these parasites results in obstruction and inflammation of lymphatics and hypertrophy of the skin and subcutaneous tissue. It is rarely observed during the first fifteen years of life, and affects mostly the legs and external genitalia. The bones are never involved. Fibrous tumors (papillomas) are absent, although ulcers, small tubercles, fissuring, and discoloration of the skin often occurs. Recurrent chills and fever are common. Merrick's affliction was of a very different character.

Merrick, in fact, suffered not from a disease but from a disorder.[25] A disease is an acquired morbid change in any tissue of an organism or in an organism as a whole; it has a specific micro-organismal source and has characteristic symptoms. A disorder, which may be either acquired or inborn, is a disturbance of structure or function or both due to a genetic defect or to a defect in the development of the embryo, or as the result of external causes such as chemical substances, injury or disease. Disease is limited to malfunctioning of the organism initiated and maintained by an infectious process. For example, tuberculosis is due to a bacillus. It is an infectious disease which may, after it has been cured, leave the individual with a disorder or malfunction of the hip. The malfunctioning hip was due to a disease, but remains a disorder. Merrick's lameness originated in tuberculosis of the hip, a disease which terminated in a permanent disorder.

A large class of disorders have no relation to disease. These are the disorders of genetic or embryological origin due to some error in the mechanisms of genetic or embryological development. For example, bleeder's disease or hemophilia, is not a disease at all, but a disorder due to a gene deficiency on an X chromosome. Extremely short or almost absent upper extremities, the condition known as phocomelia, with which thousands of European children were born in the fifties, was due to the action of the drug thalidomide which was administered to pregnant mothers during the organ-forming period of the embryo's development, between the fifth and the twelfth week. Phocomelia is clearly a disorder, not a disease.

Viruses, bacilli, and parasites cause diseases, and may leave the affected individual with a disorder, but many disorders are not caused by such agents, but are brought about by internal or external physical means.

The disorder from which Merrick suffered affected both his bones and his skin. Treves' original description of Merrick's appearance when he first encountered him in November 1884 will be found in Appendix 3. The description is nontechnical enough to present no difficulty to the reader, and requires no further comment here. In 1884-85 Treves had no more idea of the cause of Merrick's disorder than any other of his contemporary colleagues, even though, in 1882, two years before Treves came upon "the Elephant Man," it had been made the subject of a monograph. This was written by the German physician Friedrich von Recklinghausen.[26] Whether Treves ever knew of von Recklinghausen's work we do not know. Had Treves been acquainted with it it is doubtful whether he would have recognized the disorder described by von

Recklinghausen as the same as that from which Merrick suffered, for the latter's disorder was so overwhelmingly extreme it would have been difficult to associate it with the "disease" described by the German physician.

Von Recklinghausen was not the first to describe the disorder, but certainly he was the first to recognize it as a distinct clinical entity. He had no idea, and could not have had in 1882 any idea, as to its cause, but since he was the first to distinguish it as a recognizable "disease" it came to be called eponymously after him. It has been perspicaceously remarked that when a disease is named after some author, it is very likely that we do not know much about it. Today, in the matter of the disorder from which Merrick suffered, the case is very different.

Today Merrick's disorder is known as multiple neurofibromatosis or simply as neurofibromatosis. Now that the nature of the disorder is understood the eponym von Recklinghausen has increasingly come to be dropped.

Apparently there was no history of anything in the slightest resembling Merrick's disorder among his relatives. In his 1885 presentation of Merrick's condition in the *Transactions of the Pathological Society of London*, Treves states, "there was no evidence of similar deformities in any of his relatives."* In the account of Merrick's death in the *British Medical Journal*, 19 April 1890, it is repeated that "there was no family history of any similar malformation."** Neurofibromatosis often has an hereditary basis, and is usually inherited as an autosomal dominant.†[2 7] The disorder is generally transmitted from

---

*See Appendix 3.
**See Appendix 8.
†Autosomal dominant means a gene carried on one of the forty-four non-sex chromosomes, and which will always be expressed in the individual who carries it.

a parent, and as is to be expected in conditions resulting from a dominant gene, fifty percent of the children will be affected. The dominant neurofibromatosis gene is carried on one of the twenty-two pairs of chromosomes and is never carried on the sex chromosomes. A dominant gene is one that usually expresses itself in the individual who carries it on one of his non-sex chromosomes.

It is, of course, not possible to be quite certain that Merrick's disorder was without some familial hereditary component. A thoroughgoing exploration of Merrick's family history would have been difficult to make and was not attempted. Treves had, apparently, been in touch with some of Merrick's relatives shortly after he had met Merrick, for there is that reference to them in his 1885 report. Again, in the 1890 account of Merrick's death in the *British Medical Journal*, which was almost certainly based on information supplied by Treves, it is stated that "according to his relatives" Merrick had reached the age of twenty-seven at the time of his decease. The information that there was no family history of the disorder which afflicted Merrick was undoubtedly obtained from these "relatives." We know an uncle appeared and testified at the inquest held at the London Hospital on 15 April 1890. We may reasonably assume that the family history obtained was as complete as it was possible for the relatives to supply.

If, then, Merrick's disorder was not hereditary, the fact that it was congenital—that the infant was born already manifesting some of the deformities which were to develop so horribly as he grew older—suggests that we must look elsewhere for their causes.

The fact that the disorder was congenital immediately reduces the possibility that its cause was either viral, bacterial or parasitic in origin. It is highly improbable that Merrick's disorder originated from any such cause. Treves especially emphasizes the point that Merrick's general health, except for an unspecified heart condition and bronchitis, was fairly good. He exhibited no evidences of infection of any sort. If, then, his condition was due neither to a virus, a bacterium, nor a parasite, it can only have been due to some genetic defect. Genetic disorders are of two principal kinds, those affecting chromosomes and those affecting genes.

Chromosomal disorders take the form of some abnormality or abnormalities of chromosomal replication, the result of which is a loss of or an addition to the number or parts of chromosomes, or an abnormal arrangement of the chromosomes. Such chromosomal aberrations are known to produce in the body maldevelopments of every kind, depending upon the parts of the body and the particular chromosomes involved. Chromosomal aberrations usually disorder development during the organ-forming period of embryonic life, the period from the fifth to the end of the twelfth week of development. As a consequence of such chromosomally influenced disorder, the embryo or fetus is either aborted or born with more or less clearcut bodily and functional abnormalities.* Ears may be misplaced, the nose malformed, the eyes may be set too close together or are too widely separated, or the maldeveloped nose may be placed above a single eye, limbs may be malformed or incompletely developed, and so on. Virtually every tissue and organ of the body may be affected.

Such maldevelopments, due to chromosomal aberrations, have almost always been completed by the time of birth,

---

*An *embryo* is a conceptus dating from conception to the end of the eighth week of intrauterine development: a *fetus* is a conceptus dating from the beginning of the ninth week to term or delivery. A *conceptus* refers to the organism at any stage of intrauterine development.

that is to say, the basic abnormalities are more or less fully expressed. In chromosomal aberrations the malformed organs do not usually, after birth, undergo any significant change of form. Since such change did occur in Merrick, it suggests that his disorder was due not to a chromosomal aberration but to a gene mutation.

A mutation is a structural change in a gene, usually harmful, resulting in a transmissible hereditary modification in the development of a particular trait. There are three primary types of mutation: (1) point mutations which involve changes *within* the gene's molecular structure; (2) gene elimination or chromosome deficiencies; and (3) chromosome breakage. Any one of these three types of mutation may have been responsible for Merrick's disorder. Whatever type of mutation was involved, its effect was expressed in a faulty control of the growth of the cellular elements of both the skeletal and cutaneous organs of the body. Of the many varieties of cancer it is now believed that some, at least, are due to such a failure of cellular control. In some of these cancers a virus invading normal cells may produce the destructively anarchic multiplication of cells which may run wild throughout the body. In other forms of cancer the triggering mechanism may already be built into the defective genetic system. In this connection it is not without interest to note that while neurofibromatosis is, on the whole, a benign disorder, its tumors undergo a cancerous transformation, most commonly in males, in from five to ten percent of cases.

Multiple Neurofibromatosis, Neurofibromatosis, Von Recklinghausen's Disease

Multiple neurofibromatosis, von Recklinghausen's disease or neurofibromatosis, as we shall call it here, is a fairly common disorder, occurring in about 1 out of 3,000 individuals. Fifty percent of the individuals presenting the disorder are the victims of a fresh mutation arising spontaneously in them. The rate, indeed, at which spontaneous mutations for this disorder has been estimated to come into being in each generation is 1×10^{-4} per gamete (ovum or sperm)—that is, in one out of each 2,500 to 3,300 births.[28]

Neurofibromatosis occurs in many different ethnic groups, and in both sexes. In ninety-four percent of the cases there is either a loss or an increase of pigmentation with café au lait spots, most commonly on the trunk. Mental deficiency occurs in about ten percent of cases, and seizures in about twelve percent. In the more developed cases the disorder is characterized by the presence of multiple, freely hanging pedunculated tumors irregularly distributed over the skin, associated with similar tumors along the course of the deep and subcutaneous nerves. The multiple tumors are composed of fibrous or connective tissue cells and nerve fibers, and is therefore called a neurofibroma—nerve fiber tumor. Neurofibromatosis simply means the tendency to develop tumors of fibrous and nervous tissues. In most cases of neurofibromatosis the bones are not affected; in Merrick's case, however, they were.

The neurofibroma is composed of a profuse proliferation of the cells of the delicate connective tissue between the nerve fibers of a nerve trunk (endoneurium), as well as of the cells of the connective tissue sheath surrounding each bundle of fibers in a peripheral nerve (perineurium), and possibly also the connective tissue cells of the sheath surrounding a peripheral nerve (epineurium). Also involved may be the large nucleated cells which normally line the inner surface of the neurolemma—the thin membrane spirally enwrapping the fatty (myelin) layers of nerve

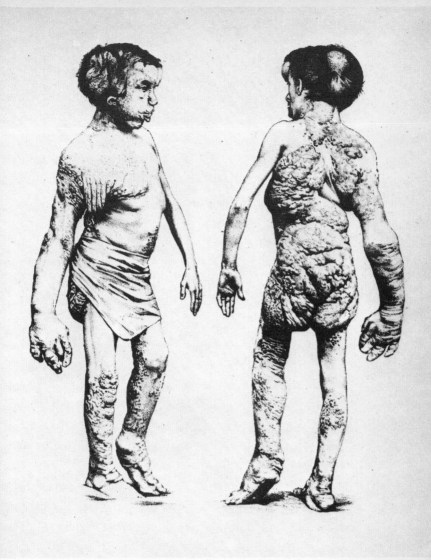

Figure 7, John Merrick as He Appeared in 1884-85 (from *The Transactions of the Pathological Society of London*, vol. 36, 1885, p. 494, Pl. xx).

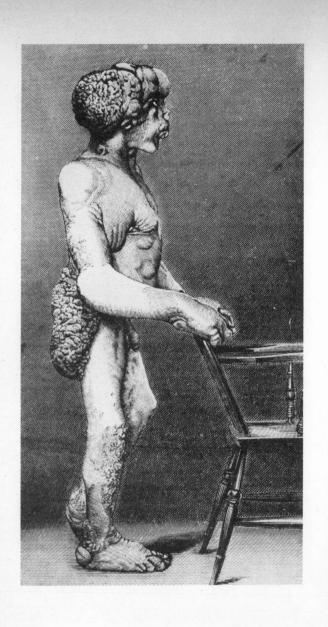

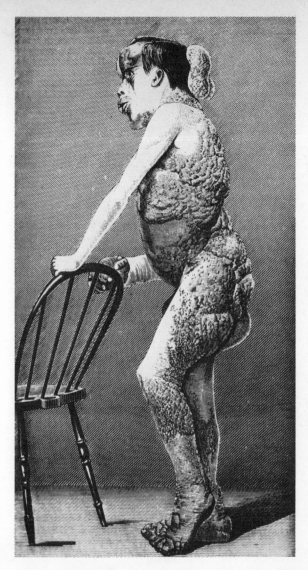

Figure 8, John Merrick in 1886 (from *The British Medical Journal*, 11 December 1886, vol. 2, p. 1189).

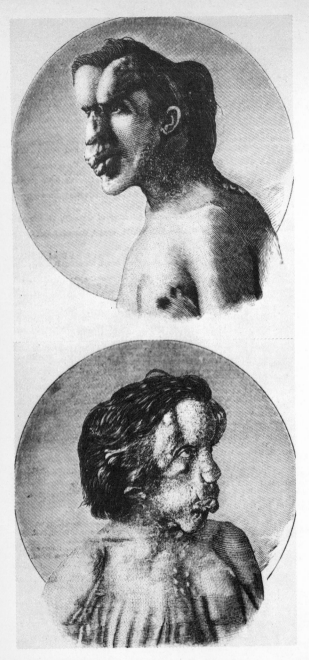

Figure 9, Head, Neck, and Upper Torso of Merrick from Photos made of Him in 1886 (from *The British Medical Journal*, 11 December 1886, vol. 2, p. 1189).

fibers and the motor portions (axons) of unmyelinated nerves. (These large nucleated cells are known as Schwann cells.) It is the wild proliferation in the skin of the cells derived from these neural tissues with many nerve fibers imbedded in their midst together with large numbers of connective tissue cells (known as Mast cells, the function of which is not understood) that produces the typical disorder of neurofibromatosis.

The primary lesion in the skin appears as an unencapsulated nodule—an irregular rounded lump—covered by pigmented epidermis. The tumors may be soft or firm and range in size from a few millimeters to diffuse growths which hang in folds from the face, neck and shoulders, all the way down to the abdomen (elephantiasis nervosum). In their undeveloped form, as noted, the tumors may be limited to a scattered half a dozen or more café au lait spots, ranging from localized nodules distributed over a particular part of the body, as on the back or forearm, to innumerable nodules of varying sizes over the greater part of the body. Hypertrophy —an enlargement— may occur in bones, and in parts of the intestinal tract, there may be rib fusion, absence of the patella. Neurofibromata may invade various organs, and there may be fibrosing of the alveolar cells of the lungs. Even though it is disfiguring, neurofibromatosis is usually benign. In cases of spinal cord involvement or the development of a malignant and metastasizing tumor (Schwannoma), death is the inevitable consequence.

John Merrick's Skin And Bone Lesions

The illustrations showing Merrick's appearance (figs. 7 to 9) require few words. Fig. 7 shows Merrick at the time when Treves first met him in November 1884. This

illustration represents an engraving made from a photograph. It was published as part of Treves' report on
Merrick in the *Transactions of the Pathological Society of
London* in 1885. At this time Merrick was in his
twenty-second or twenty-third year. As will be seen from
this illustration, virtually every part of Merrick's body was
affected by the disorder, with the exception of the left
upper extremity and shoulder. The latter was perfectly
normal in every respect, and remained so throughout his
life, as may be seen from the cast of Merrick's forearm and
hand taken after his death (fig. 10). The skeletal elements
forming the upper extremity were also perfectly normally
formed.

Quite otherwise is the gross overgrowth and malformation of every part of the right upper extremity (figs. 11
and 12). This also appears to be somewhat longer than the
left extremity. In addition to the overgrowth of bone and
soft tissue the greater apparent elongation was due to the
extreme curvature of the spine to the right from which
Merrick suffered, as may be seen in figs. 26 and 27.
Merrick's right hand was completely useless to him. The
fingers were so deformed and the palm so overgrown with
fibrous tissue and disordered elements of the subcutaneous
tissues, that it could at most have served only as a sort of
anchor. For all practical purposes his left hand had to serve
him for two. It was with this one left hand that Merrick
wove his baskets and made his remarkable models. All the
bones of the right upper extremity were more or less
affected by the disorder (fig. 13). The humerus is
thickened, and at its jointure with the radius and ulna is
much deformed. The forearm bones show the ulna to be
badly affected while the radius (on the thumb side) is
much less affected.

That the skin was involved wherever the underlying

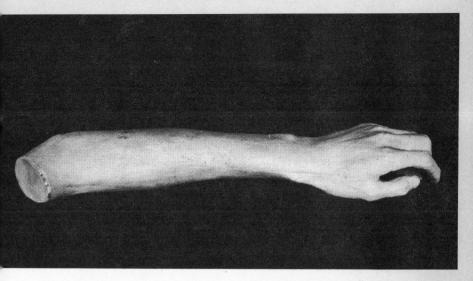

Figure 10, Cast of the Left Forearm and Hand.

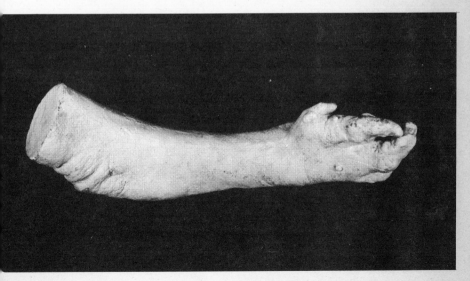

Figure 11, Cast of the Right Forearm and Hand.

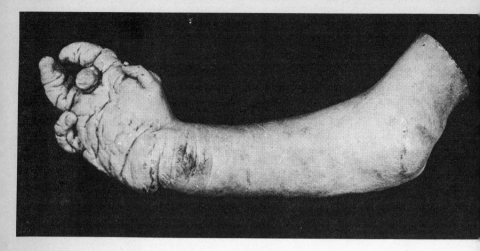

Figure 12, Cast of the Palm of the Right Hand and Flexor Surface of Forearm and Elbow.

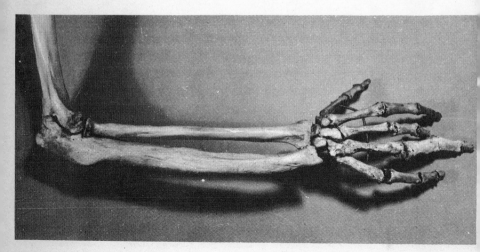

Figure 13, Bones of the Right Elbow Joint, Forearm, and Hand.

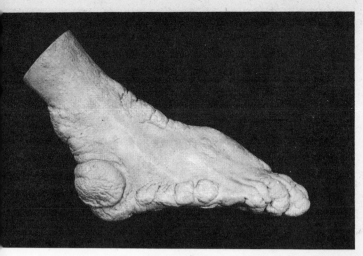

Figure 14, Cast of the Right Foot. Outer View.

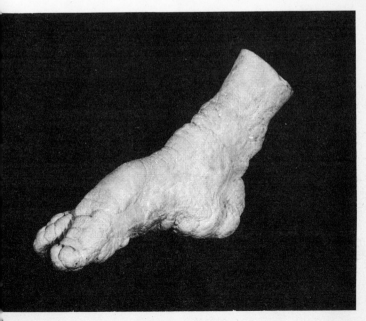

Figure 15, Cast of the Right Foot. Inner View.

Figure 16, John Merrick as He Appeared Some Months Before His Death (from *The British Medical Journal*, vol. 1, 1890, p. 916).

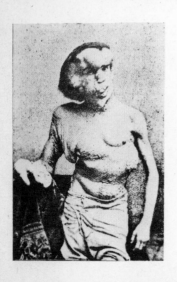

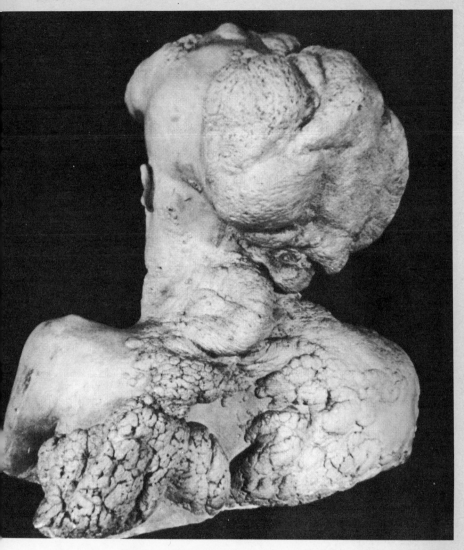

Figure 17, Postmortem Cast of the Back of the Head, Neck, and Shoulders.

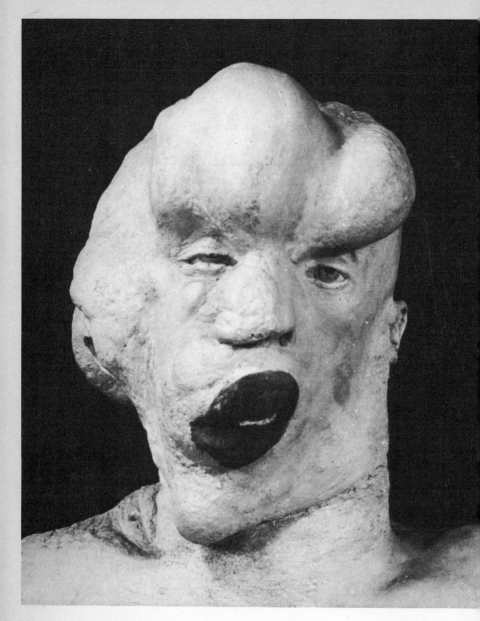

Figure 18, Postmortem Cast of the Head and Neck. Facial View.

bones were also disordered presents an interesting and significant correlation. Sheathed (myelinated) and unsheathed (unmyelinated) nerves enter a bone along with the blood vessels that supply it. The nerve fibers can often be traced as far as the bone-forming cells. Wherever the connective tissue cells surrounding the nerve bundles, between the nerve fibers, and around the peripheral nerves (myelin sheaths) were pathologically affected, the bone became disordered. It is this fact that presumably accounts for the close skeletal and skin association of the disorder that affected Merrick.

Returning to Merrick's appearance in 1884-85, as shown in fig. 7, we observe the massive bosses (elevations) on his forehead, due to the underlying enormous overgrowths of bone, and the growths at the back and side of his head, involving on the right side the ear, jaw, and neck. Hanging from below his shoulder, on the right side, in front of his armpit, are several massive folds of skin. Opposite the fold on his right arm there is a growth of numerous tubercles. Both legs also show an extensive distribution of such tubercles. The feet are badly deformed and exhibit a considerable overgrowth of massive tubercles. These are best seen in the casts, taken at the time of Merrick's death (figs. 14 and 15). The malformation and size of his feet required the sewing of specially made boots.

The apparent clubfoot on the left side was principally due to disease of the hip and thighbone. This caused Merrick to walk with a marked limp, and disabled him from standing long without support. The diffuse lobulated tumors which covered the back and buttocks appear to have progressively worsened, as may be judged from the photographs made in 1886 (figs. 8 and 9) and late in 1889 (fig. 16), a few months before Merrick's death. The papillomas which covered Merrick's body are branching or lobulated benign tumors derived from the layer of cells which covers the internal and external surfaces of the body, including vessels and cavities. Such cells are known as epithelial cells, and the tumors associated with them generally involve glands and related structures. The odor which Treves mentions as emanating from Merrick's skin was undoubtedly derived from the secretions of the innumerable disordered sebaceous and sweat glands disseminated throughout these tumors. With the limited opportunities for bathing Merrick enjoyed prior to his rehabilitation, the accumulated bacterial decomposition of the secretions from the sweat and sebaceous glands would have given him a nauseating odor. This, too, must have added to Merrick's misery. The regular baths he was able to take following his settlement in his new hospital quarters, completely eliminated this odor, thus indicating that it was in no way due to some abnormality of the sweat and sebaceous glands themselves.

The external genitalia, penis, scrotum, and testes, appear to have been entirely normal and free of any form of disorder (see fig. 8). This would independently tend to confirm Treves' statement that Merrick's "bodily deformity had left unmarred the instincts and feelings of his years. He was amorous. He would have liked to have been a lover." It was, alas, an experience Merrick was never to know.

A much clearer view of the tumors affecting the back and right side of the head, the back of the neck, and the back may be obtained from the photograph of the cast of these areas made immediately after his death (fig. 17). As may be seen from this closeup view, no area is actually free of involvement, with the exception of the upper part of the left shoulder, and a small portion of the left scalp.

The delicately sculptured left ear remained almost

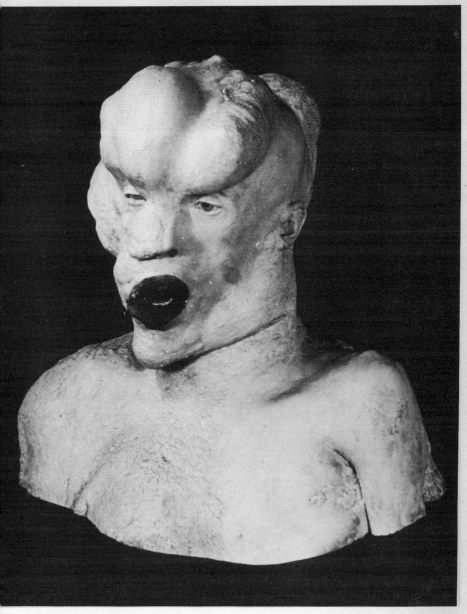

Figure 19, Postmortem Three-Quarter View From the Left of the Head, Neck, and Torso.

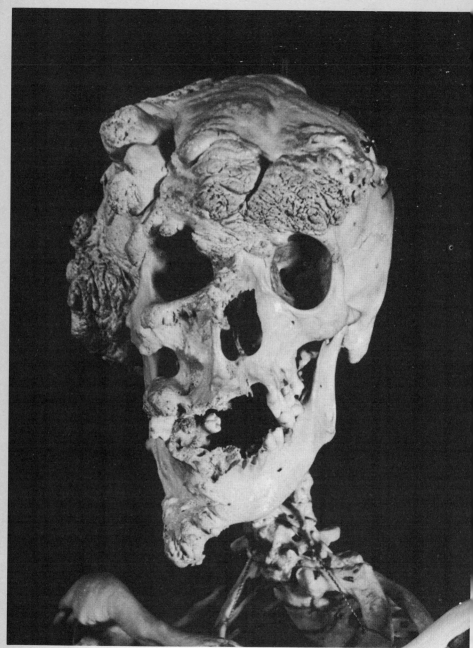

Figure 20, Frontal View of the Skull.

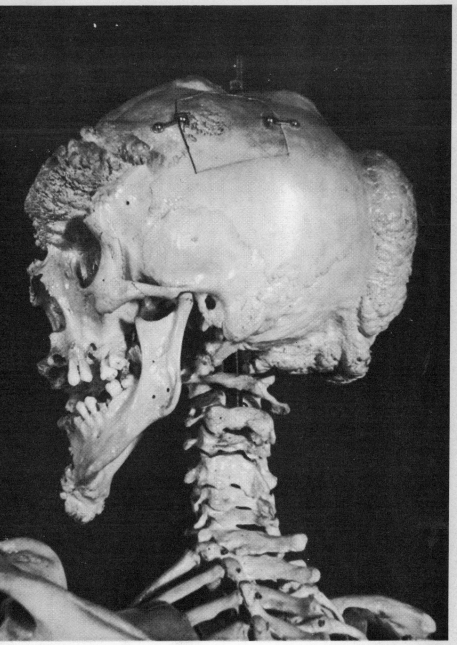

Figure 21, Left Side View of the Skull.

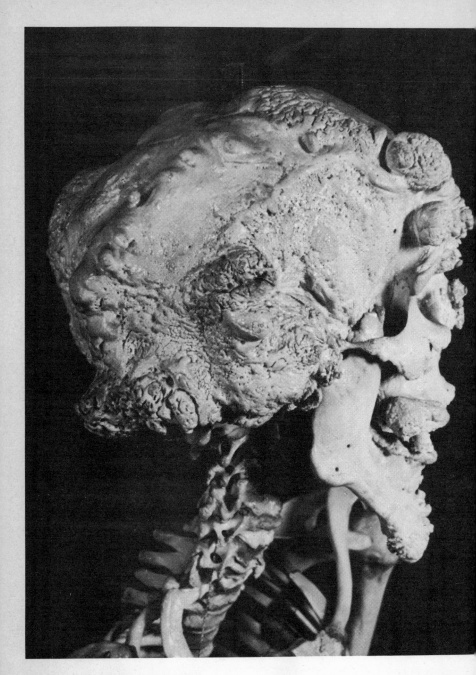

Figure 22, Right Side View of the Skull.

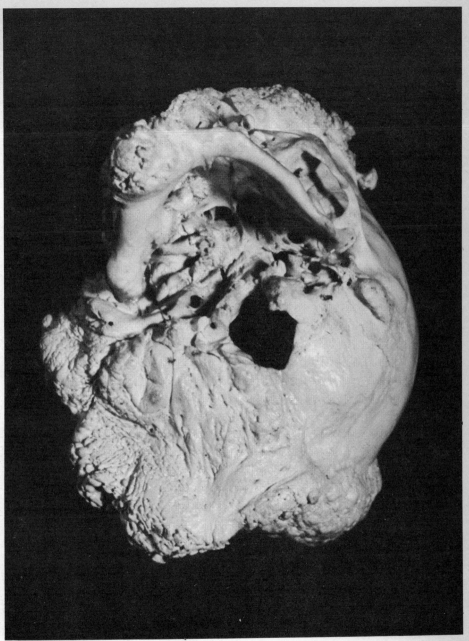

Figure 23, Base of the Skull. Three-Quarter View From the Back.

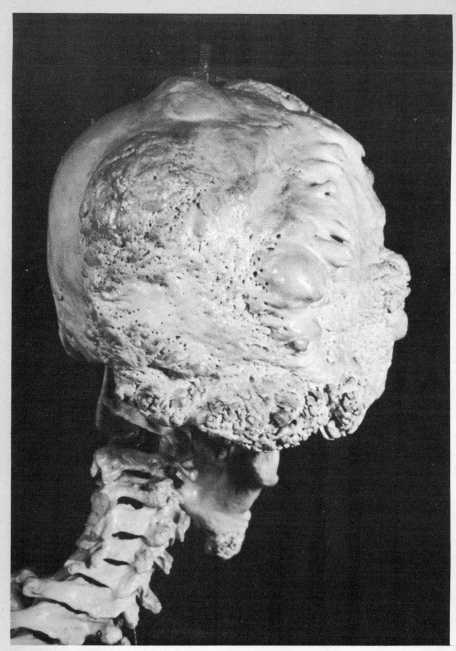

Figure 24, Three-Quarter View of the Neck and Right Side of the Skull.

completely uninvolved—it seems to have been affected at
the ear lobe, which was not free but attached to the side of
the head—but as the disorder progressed the right ear was
rotated, deformed, and almost completely engulfed by the
enormous tumorous overgrowth (figs. 18, 19, and 23).
Hearing on the right side was probably considerably
reduced, if it existed at all.

From figs. 18 and 19, showing the cast of Merrick's head
and shoulders in frontal and three-quarter view, it will be
seen that the only normal-appearing part of his head was a
part of the left side of the scalp, and left face from the
upper eyelid, excluding the lips to the lower jaw. The
unaffected part of the scalp was in life covered with a mass
of brown hair. After death this was shaven in order to
make the cast. As would be expected, the only underlying
bony elements on this left side of the head and face which
are not affected are those entering into the formation of
the "cheekbone" (maxilla, zygomatic, zygomatic process
of the temporal), the temporal bone, the great wing of the
sphenoid, the squama of the temporal, and the parts of the
frontal and parietal bones above the squama (figs. 20 and
21).

This continued correlation of unaffected underlying
bone with unaffected overlying cutaneous structures,
together with the equally marked association of disordered
underlying bone with disordered overlying integument
indicates strongly that the disorder spread along the course
of the connective tissue cells of the nerve sheaths and
those between and around the nerve fibers originating
from the same main nerve trunks or branches. The
forehead, face, and jaws of the right side were the result of
the disorder spreading along the course of the ophthalmic,
maxillary, and mandibular divisions of the trigeminal
(fifth) nerve and its branches (figs. 20 and 22). On the

right side every part of the face is affected, including the
upper and lower eyelids, the infraorbital region, the nose
beyond the midline, the maxillary, and the mandibular
areas.

To the right of the midline of the lower jaw a great bony
tumor grew from its body (figs. 22 to 24). This served to
pull the overlying soft tissues and the lips toward the right,
as may be seen in fig. 18. A tumorous growth from the
right upper jaw and palate (figs. 20 and 22) further served
to deform the tooth-bearing portions of the upper and
lower jaws, and since, as a consequence of these tumors,
the jaws could not be properly closed, the vertical portion
of the lower jaw (the ramus), on this right side especially
has undergone considerable elongation, and the molar
teeth some displacement and rotation (figs. 20 and 21). On
the left side the upper and lower jaws are unaffected by
tumorous growths, but there has been some thinning of
the bone and rotation of the molar teeth in the upper jaw.
Eating at best could not have been easy for Merrick, and
chewing must always have remained a problem. And until
they were removed surgically, the fibrous growths from his
palate must seriously have interfered with his ability to
masticate his food and to swallow. His teeth seem to have
been singularly free of cavities.

Figs. 22 to 25 show the back, right side, base, and top of
the skull together with the enormous overgrowth of bone
reflected in the overgrowth of skin in the corresponding
areas.

Fig. 23 shows the base of the skull. Here the great
tumorous growth of the right side of the lower jaw may be
seen, and also the manner in which not only the lower jaw
has been rotated to the right, but also the greater part of
the base of the skull.

Figs. 26 and 27 show the front and back views of the

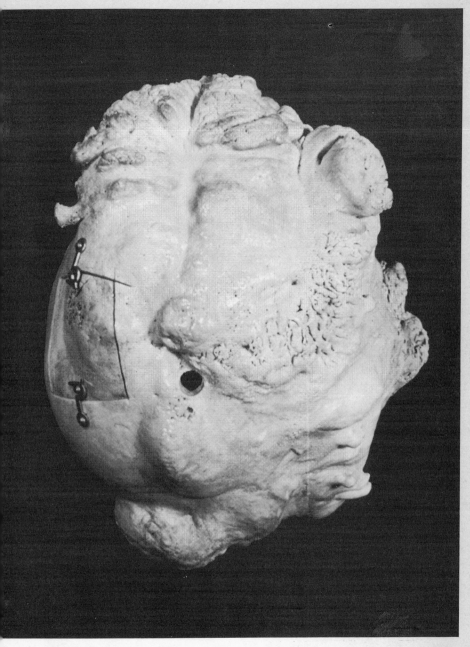

Figure 25, The Top of the Skull. The Back of the Skull Is Toward the Bottom of the Page.

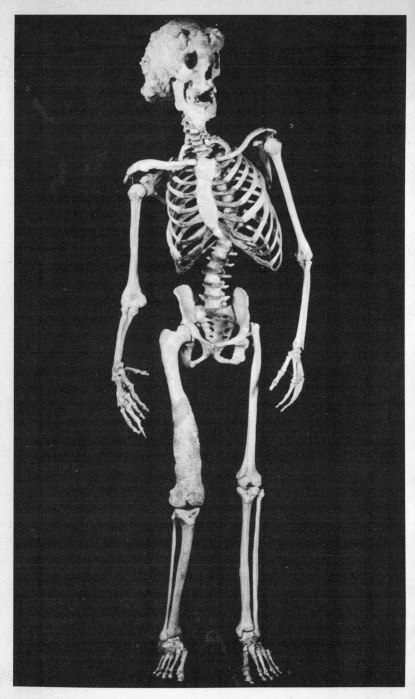

Figure 26, The Skeleton of John Merrick, Frontal View.

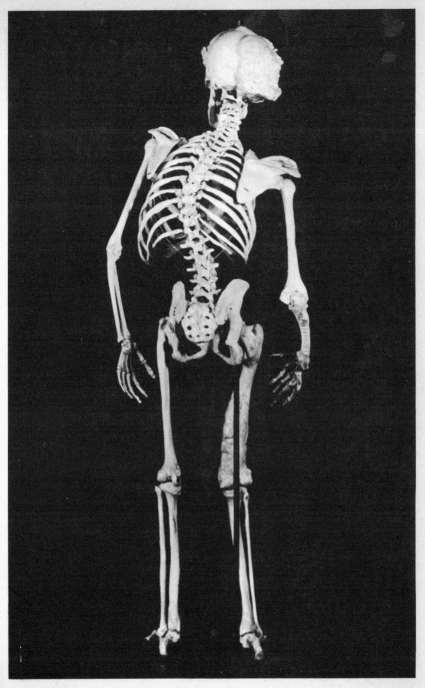

Figure 27, The Skeleton of John Merrick. Back View.

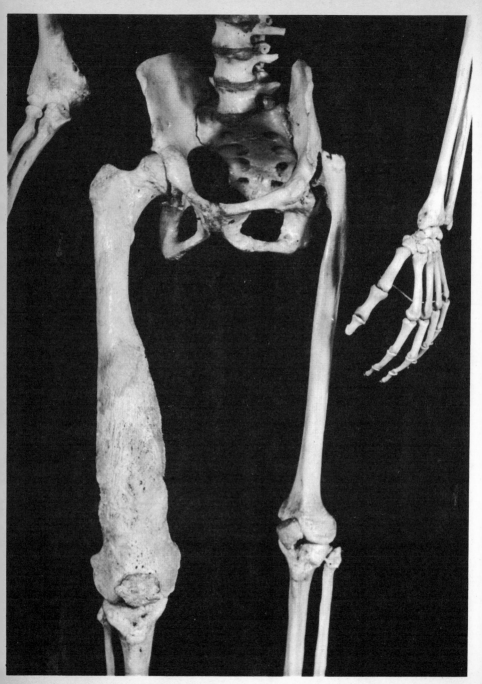

Figure 28, Pelvis, Thigh-Bones, and Knee Joint.

complete skeleton. From these views it may be seen that the only normal bones in the whole body of Merrick, were the bones of the left upper extremity, shoulder girdle, and most of the ribs—all on the left side. The only bone on the right side which seems to have been unaffected is the shoulder blade at the back.

The curvature (scoliosis) of the spine is markedly to the left. Almost all the vertebrae are to some extent affected by the disorder. The hip bones are quite misshapen. The right thigh bone is badly disordered and overgrown, especially in its lower two-thirds, while on the left the thigh bone is thinned out, and has lost its head to the disease of the hip-joint in which the socket (acetabulum) wherein the head of the thigh bone normally lodges is also virtually obliterated. It was disease of the left hip-joint which was largely responsible for Merrick's disabling limp. The asymmetry and different lengths of the bones of the right and left lower limbs will be evident from figs. 26 to 28.

In fig. 28 may be seen a closer view of the pelvis, thigh-bones, and knee joints, together with the right elbow joint, and the forearm and handbones of the left upper extremity. The only normal bones are of this left upper extremity.

Chapter 5

Conclusion

Man, in the unsearchable darkness, knoweth one thing,
That as he is, so was he made.
Robert Bridges, *The Testament of Beauty*

It is, perhaps, more important to have told the story of John Merrick, "the Elephant Man," than to inquire into the conditions that made him what he was. No one who reads that story can be anything but moved, even ennobled. As he was, so was John Merrick made. But what were the influences that made him what he was? There, some may say, lies the mystery. Mystery there will always remain. It is difficult to circumnavigate the human soul or even define it. It is, perhaps, more important to be able to understand it than to define it. This we have attempted to do in the preceding pages.

A sub-microscopic mutation in an hereditary particle, a gene, caused Merrick to develop a disfiguringly hideous disorder which would make him an outcast among men. Chance caused him to be born into a poor family. Since he was already deformed at birth and grew increasingly more so, he might have been abandoned while he was still a small infant. But he was not. As we have seen, there seems to be good ground for believing that he received much love from his mother during the first three or four years of his life. It was in large part this humanizing experience, we have argued, that provided him with the basic strength that enabled him to sustain himself and to surmount all the handicaps from which he suffered, and to bear with courage and without complaint the martyrdom which was his lot every moment of the day.

This side of the grave Merrick had neither hope nor expectation of relief from the miserable conditions of his life. His situation was in every sense desperate, his physical agony exceeded only by his mental torment, a despised creature for whom there could be no consolation of any kind. To live with the reality of his physical hideousness, his incapacitating deformities, and the unremitting pain was more than trial enough, but to be exposed to the cruelly lacerating expressions of horror and disgust by all who beheld him, was, one may suppose, even more difficult to bear. And yet, in order to survive, Merrick had to force himself to suffer these humiliations by exposing himself to the crowds who paid to gape and yawp at this freak of nature, "the Elephant Man."

Never being able to venture out normally in the light of day, living the most ignominious existence, shifting from one manager and "impresario" to another, constantly on the move, badgered by the police, entirely alone in the world, knowing that there was to be no surcease, no amelioration of his condition, Merrick's hold on life, tenuous as it was, never weakened. His spirit remained invincible to the end.

He could, at any time, have cut the slender thread by which his life hung, but he chose to live. No matter what further bludgeonings Fate might have in store for him,

Merrick was all the more resolved to go on. It were as if he had said to himself, "I suffer, therefore I am. And I am what I am because I suffer." It was, we believe, a conscious decision, at which he had arrived quite early in life, to live his life with the dignity of a man, to stand as erectly as he was able, and while the light from the pure flame that burned within him flickered, he would keep the faith with himself.

"Life is a pure flame, and we live by an invisible Sun within us." The words are from *Hydrotaphia* (1658) by Sir Thomas Browne (1605-1682) who, in another of his books, *Religio Medici* (1642), wrote the words which John Merrick might well have uttered to himself, "Not that I am ashamed of the Anatomy of my parts, or can accuse nature for playing the bungler in any part of me, whereby I might not call my selfe as wholesome a morsell for the wormes as any."[29] But unlike Sir Thomas Browne, John Merrick counted not the world a hospital to die in, but a wretched rack upon which the imprisoned human spirit, however tormented, whatever the mortal coils that hemmed it in, seeks invincibly to express itself.

One of the things we may learn concerning the nature of human nature from the story of John Merrick is that given the adequate material to work on—that is, the genetic potentials—the love that the infant receives during its first three years is fundamental for its subsequent healthy development. One may express the doubt that Merrick would have come through as well as he did without the favoring genetic potentials.

Yet making every allowance for the genes upon which his experience had to work, we would nonetheless maintain that the love that John Merrick received from his mother as an infant constituted the principal influence in enabling him to respond to the challenges of his troubled life as successfully, even triumphantly, as he did.

In the love he received from his mother Merrick may

well have had the advantage over Alexander Pope. Pope's deformities were as nothing compared with those from which John Merrick suffered. His success as a renowned poet, his wit and wealth enabled him to live in comfort and move in whatever circles he chose. There could hardly have been a greater contrast in the conditions in which each of these men lived. And yet, Pope, as a humane being, was virtually destroyed by his preoccupation with his physical infirmities, while Merrick managed to live with his far greater handicaps without being corroded by them. The genes that enabled Pope to become a great poet were insufficient to enable him to become a great man, to rise above his physical infirmities and go on with the business of life, to be, to do, and to depart gracefully.

But, as we have argued, perhaps it is this very contrast between the conditions of their lives that made it easier for Merrick to make the pact with himself that nothing more in this world could hurt him, and that he would make the best of his lot as well as he knew how. The contrast between his own physical condition and the condition of his everyday life was all of a piece and nowhere nearly as marked as in the case of Pope. Contrast emphasizes difference, and the difference between what Pope knew himself to be physically and what he was as a poet, man of genius, and indeed the foremost poet, the most sought-after literary lion of his day, was something with which he perhaps could never come to terms.

There have been other writers who have suffered from physical handicaps. Remy de Gourmont suffered from a disfiguring facial skin disorder. So did Sinclair Lewis. Remy de Gourmont solved his problem by seldom leaving his chambers. Sinclair Lewis attempted to deal with his with irascibility and alcohol. Toulouse-Lautrec, who was a dwarf, embarked upon a life of systematic self-destruction.

It seems to be the case that men of great gifts generally

find the contrast between their physical handicaps and their social acclaim unmanageably difficult to handle. In this sense John Merrick was lucky, in that there was little contrast between his physical handicaps and the conditions of his daily life.

Following his rescue by Treves the contrast between his former way of life and the life he was enjoying in the hospital could contribute only to Merrick's sense almost of ecstasy. "I am happy every hour of the day" is how he put it—and all those who had a part in the making of Treves himself must have been happy, too: the shades of William Barnes, Treves' parents, and some of his teachers.

What is the moral of this story, if it has one? It is that the influence of a really good person lives on in the benefits he confers upon others, that that influence never really fades, and that courage and integrity are among the supreme virtues of humanity, outlasting even death itself.

Appendix 1

Under "Reports of Societies," Pathological Society of London, Tuesday, 2 December 1884. *The British Medical Journal*, 6 December 1884, p. 1140.

Congenital Deformity—Mr. TREVES showed a man who presented an extraordinary appearance, owing to a series of deformities, some congenital exostoses of the skull; extensive papillomatous growths and large pendulous masses in connection with the skin; great enlargement of the right upper limb, involving all the bones. From the massive distortion of the head, and the extensive areas covered by papillomatous growth, the patient had been called "the elephant-man."

Appendix 2

Under "Reports of Societies," Pathological Society of London, Tuesday, 17 March 1885. *The British Medical Journal*, 21 March 1885, p. 595.

Congenital Deformity—Mr. F. TREVES gave a description, illustrated by photographs, of the case of the so-called elephant man, who had been previously shown to the Society (BRITISH MEDICAL JOURNAL, December 6, 1884, page 1140). The deformity of the skin was twofold; in the first place, there was an increase in the subcutaneous cellular tissues; this was so extreme in the right pectoral region and at the buttocks, as to lead to the formation of pendulous masses; further, certain parts of the skin were also affected with congenital papillomatous tumours. The bones of the skull were deformed and overgrown, so that the circumference of the head was so greatly increased as to be equal with that of his waist. There was a hypertrophic deformity not only of the cranial and facial bones, but of the bones of the upper limb, and the bones of the feet; the enlargement of the facial bones and the bones of the upper limb was confined to one side.—Dr. H. R. CROCKER, thought that the case belonged to the same class of cases as dermatolysis and

what similar case, but without papillomatous growths. The
association between pachydermatocoele and papillomatous
growths had been before pointed out, but the occurrence
of changes in the bones had not, he believed been
previously observed.

Appendix 3

Treves' First Full Report of Merrick's Disorder in *The Transactions of the Pathological Society of London*, vol. xxxvi, 1885, pp. 494-498.

7. A Case of Congenital Deformity.

By Frederick Treves.

[Fig. 7]

The subject of this deformity was a man aged 24, who earned a living by exhibiting himself as "the Elephant Man." He was a little below the average height and was lame by reason of a shortening of the left leg that had followed an attack of hip disease in childhood. The deformity concerned both the cutaneous and osseous systems. With regard to the skin the affected districts showed a twofold abnormality. In the first place over certain regions the subcutaneous tissue was greatly increased in amount. From this it followed that the integument in such regions was raised considerably above the surrounding normal skin. It was also rendered remarkably loose, so that it could be freely slid about, and if grasped it could be drawn away from the deeper parts in immense folds. In three places the skin so affected had assumed the form of a pendulous flap. Thus from the right pectoral region immediately in front of the axilla a great flap of loose flabby skin hung vertically downwards. It measured six inches in vertical height and about the same in breadth. A smaller, firmer, and much less conspicuous fold existed also at the posterior aspect of the right axilla. The integument over both buttocks was continued downwards as a huge thick flap which reached almost to the level of the middle of the thigh. So solid and extensive was this flap that it appeared at first to be the buttock itself, and its existence somewhat interfered with the act of defecation.

The second species of abnormality met with in the skin took the form of a papillomatous condition of its surface. The parts so involved presented the appearance of an ordinary congenital papilloma of the skin when met with in an adult. This condition of the surface, when added to the abnormality of the subcutaneous tissue already alluded to, produced a most remarkable appearance in the involved districts. The papillomatous growth was far more exuberant in some places than in others. Thus over the right pectoral region the individual abnormal papillae were comparatively small, and the general surface even. Towards the right clavicle the papillomatous condition passed off into a mere roughening of the integument. In other parts, viz. on the front of the abdomen, at the back of the neck, and over the right popliteal space the papillomatous growth was also small, the individual elevations being of no great magnitude. Over the dorsal region, and especially over the gluteal districts, this peculiar growth was met with in its most exuberant condition. The individual papillary tumours were large, the sulci between them deep, and the whole mass here and there broken up into deep fissures and clefts. The colour of the skin over the involved districts was normal save over the most prominent masses and dependent parts, where it was dusky or purplish. From the larger of the growths an exceedingly foul odour arose akin to that met with in smaller papillomata.

The whole of the integument of the body was involved in one way or another, with the exception of the following parts: the ears, the eyelids, portions of the face, the whole of the left upper extremity, a patch below the right scapula, and another of smaller size over the left buttock, nearly the whole of the front of the abdomen, and of the right thigh, the front of the left thigh and left leg, and the back of the right leg. The integument of both feet was grossly deformed.

It is remarkable that the skin of the penis and scrotum was perfectly normal in every respect. In no part was there any naevoid growth. In some places, as for example over the front of the abdomen and the right pectoral region, the papilloma existed without any other abnormality, without the thickening of the subcutaneous tissue that was so marked in other districts. On the other hand there were regions where the chief or only deformity depended upon extreme thickening of the connective tissue under the skin, the integument itself being approximately normal. This condition was met with in the right forearm and in parts of the right hand and the feet, and upon the scalp. There were papillary growths over the greater part of the face, but none upon any portion of the hairy scalp. The growths upon the skin followed no distinct areas of distribution. They appeared to be scattered about casually or accidentally, and to be influenced by no specific anatomical arrangement.

The deformities of the osseous system were limited to

the skull, the right upper extremity, and the feet. The proportions of the head were enormously increased and its general outline that of a hydrocephalic skull. The surface of the skull was so irregular as to render any detailed description very difficult. It was covered by huge rounded exostoses, the chief of which were larger than a large Tangerine orange. The most conspicuous of these bossy masses of bone were placed upon the frontal bone, the posterior parts of the parietals, and the upper part of the occipital bone. Apart from these large exostoses the right side of the cranium just about and behind the ear appeared to bulge outwards with the result that the upper part of the pinna was folded downwards. In the intervals between the more conspicuous exostoses the surface of the skull was not regular, but presented ridges and irregular upheavals of bone that disregarded sutures and were disposed in a perfectly chaotic manner. Indeed, the whole head was ostentatiously unsymmetrical. From the upper part of the right side of the frontal bone a very large ridge took origin and ran backwards almost horizontally across the vertex until it became lost among the elevations over the hinder part of the parietal bone. Neither the orbit nor the meatus had been encroached upon on either side. There was no paralysis of any cranial nerve, and the patient had presented no evidences of epilepsy or other cerebral disturbance. He never suffered from headache and his intelligence was by no means of a low order. The chief exostoses, and especially those in the occipital region, were covered with scalp tissue that presented a great thickening of its subcutaneous layers, and by this hypertrophy the prominence of the tumour was much increased. Over the frontal excrescences was thickened integument covered by a papillary growth. The right superior maxillary bone was greatly and irregularly enlarged. The right side of the hard palate and the right upper teeth occupied a lower level than the corresponding parts of the left side. By reason of this growth of the bone the nose had been turned to the left side and the lips rendered unduly prominent. From the front part of the right upper jaw a connective-tissue growth had developed, which, projecting beyond the mouth, had prevented him from closing his lips and had interfered with mastication and articulation. This had been removed at the Leicester Infirmary two years ago. The lower jaw and the other facial bones appeared normal.

In the right upper extremity every bone was found hypertrophied with the exception of the clavicle and scapula.

The whole limb appeared two or three times the size of its fellow. The hypertrophy in the bones was quite regular, and no exostoses could be found. The fingers were grossly misshaped. All the phalangeal bones were enlarged and covered by greatly thickened soft parts and rugose hypertrophied skin. All the nails were perfect, but some of the phalangeal joints had become partially dislocated by reason of the irregular character of the hypertrophy. The member presented no trace of oedema. He had good use of the right shoulder and elbow, pronation and supination were performed with difficulty, and the movements at the wrist and in the fingers were so imperfect that the hand was almost useless. He could, however, dress and feed himself without assistance. Both feet were in almost the same condition as the right hand, the bones being enlarged and the toes misshaped and of enormous size.

The man was a native of Leicester. He had no brothers or sister, and there was no evidence of similar deformities in any of his relatives. He gave an elaborate story of a fright his mother had received shortly before his birth from having been knocked down by an elephant in a circus.

From his own account it would appear that his head, his right arm, and his feet have always been grossly deformed. He states, however, that when a child his skin was simply thickened, loose, and rough, and that the main papillary growths were not present. There is distinct evidence to show that these latter growths are at present extending rapidly. Moreover, the hypertrophy of the soft tissues of the fingers has so increased of late as to greatly diminish the already limited movements of the hand. The man enjoys good health, has suffered from no serious illnesses, and possesses a fair degree of muscular strength.

March 17th, 1885.

Appendix 4

Mr. Carr Gomm's Letter to *The Times* (London), published Saturday, 4 December 1886, p. 6.

"The Elephant Man."

To the Editor of the Times

Sir,—I am authorized to ask your powerful assistance in bringing to the notice of the public the following most exceptional case. There is now in a little room off one of our attic wards a man named Joseph Merrick, aged about 27, a native of Leicester, so dreadful a sight that he is unable even to come out by daylight to the garden. He has been called "the elephant man" on account of his terrible deformity. I will not shock your readers with any detailed description of his infirmities, but only one arm is available for work.

Some 18 month ago, Mr. Treves, one of the surgeons of the London Hospital, saw him as he was exhibited in a room off the Whitechapel-road. The poor fellow was then covered by an old curtain, endeavouring to warm himself over a brick which was heated by a lamp. As soon as a

110

sufficient number of pennies had been collected by the manager at the door, poor Merrick threw off his curtain and exhibited himself in all his deformity. He and the manager went halves in the net proceeds of his exhibition, until at last the police stopped the exhibition of his deformities as against public decency. Unable to earn his livelihood by exhibiting himself any longer in England, he was persuaded to go over to Belgium, where he was taken in hand by an Austrian, who acted as his manager. Merrick managed in this way to save a sum of nearly £50, but the police there too kept him moving on, so that his life was a miserable and hunted one. One day, however, when the Austrian saw that the exhibition was pretty well played out, he decamped with poor Merrick's hardly-saved capital of £50, and left him alone and absolutely destitute in a foreign country. Fortunately, however, he had something to pawn, by which he raised sufficient money to pay his passage back to England, for he felt that the only friend he had in the world was Mr. Treves, of the London Hospital. He therefore, though with much difficulty, made his way there, for at every station and landing-place the curious crowd so thronged and dogged his steps that it was not an easy matter for him to get about. When he reached the London Hospital he had only the clothes in which he stood. He has been taken in by our hospital, though there is, unfortunately, no hope of his cure, and the question now arises what is to be done with him in the future.

He has the greatest horror of the workhouse, nor is it possible, indeed, to send him into any place where he could not insure privacy, since his appearance is such that all shrink from him.

The Royal Hospital for Incurables and the British Home for Incurables both decline to take him in, even if sufficient funds were forthcoming to pay for him.

The police rightly prevent his being personally exhibited again; he cannot go out into the streets, as he is everywhere so mobbed that existence is impossible; he cannot, in justice to others, be put in the general ward of a workhouse, and from such, even if possible, he shrinks with the greatest horror; he ought not to be detained in our hospital (where he is occupying a private ward, and being treated with the greatest kindness—he says he has never before known in his life what quiet and rest were), since his case is incurable, and not suited, therefore, to our overcrowded general hospital; the incurable hospitals refuse to take him in even if we paid for him in full, and the difficult question therefore remains what is to be done for him.

Terrible though his appearance is, so terrible indeed that women and nervous persons fly in terror from the sight of him, and that he is debarred from seeking to earn his livelihood in any ordinary way, yet he is superior in intelligence, can read and write, is quiet, gentle, not to say even refined in his mind. He occupies his time in the hospital by making with his one available hand little cardboard models, which he sends to the matron, doctor, and those who have been kind to him. Through all the miserable vicissitudes of his life he has carried about a painting of his mother to show that she was a decent and presentable person, and as a memorial of the only one who was kind to him in life until he came under the kind care of the nursing staff of the London Hospital and the surgeon who has befriended him.

It is a case of singular affliction brought about through no fault of himself; he can but hope for quiet and privacy during a life which Mr. Treves assures me is not likely to be long.

Can any of your readers suggest to me some fitting place

where he can be received? And then I feel sure that, when that is found, charitable people will come forward and enable me to provide him with such accommodation. In the meantime, though it is not the proper place for such an incurable case, the little room under the roof of our hospital and out of Cotton Ward supplies him with all he wants. The Master of the Temple on Advent Sunday preached an eloquent sermon on the subject of our Master's answer to the question, "Who did sin, this man or his parents, that he was born blind?" showing how one of the Creator's objects in permitting men to be born to a life of hopeless and miserable disability was that the works of God should be manifested in evoking the sympathy and kindly aid of those on whom such a heavy cross is not laid.

Some 76,000 patients a year pass through the doors of our hospital, but I have never before been authorized to invite public attention to any particular case, so it may well be believed that this case is exceptional.

Any communication about this should be addressed either to myself or to the secretary at the London Hospital.

I have the honour to be, Sir, yours obediently,

F.C. CARR GOMM, Chairman London Hospital.
November 30.

Appendix 5

The 1886 Account of "The Elephant Man" in *The British Medical Journal*, 11 December 1886, pp. 1188-1189.

The "Elephant-Man."

A letter from Mr. Carr Gomm, Chairman of the London Hospital, appeared last week in the *Times*. It contained an appeal to the charitable public on behalf of John Merrick, a man afflicted by so terrible a deformity that he cannot venture out by daylight to the garden of the hospital. Not only does his condition prevent him from being kept in a general ward or admitted into an institution for incurables, but he cannot even travel by public conveyances. Among other experiences of this kind, acutely painful to his feelings, a steamboat captain refused on one occasion to take him as a passenger.

Most medical men who read the letter must have naturally concluded, provided that they were not in possession of certain facts, that this unhappy man is the subject of elephantiasis. It turns out, however, that his case has been twice before the Pathological Society of London. The first notice appeared in the JOURNAL of December 6th, 1884; the second in our issue of March 21st, 1885;

and the case was fully reported in the Society's *Transactions* (vol.xxxvi, 1885, page 494) as "A Case of Congenital Deformity," and figured at Plate xx [Fig. 7].

Since that plate was taken, the disease has made great progress. Through the kindness of Mr. Treves, we have been supplied with four photographs, representing the patient's present condition. A comparison of these drawings with the plate above noted will show how the disease has advanced during the past two years.

The "elephant-man" is a native of Leicester, and is about twenty-seven years of age. He earned his living at one time by exhibiting himself under the name which he still bears—a name not meant to imply elephantiasis, but bestowed on him on account of the bony exostoses on his frontal bone. This, combined with a deformity of the superior maxilla which gives a trunk-like appearance to the nose and upper lip, causes the profile of the face to remind the observer of the profile of an elephant's head.

Mr. Treves discovered him about two years ago, when he was exhibited in a room off the Whitechapel Road. The police stopped this degrading exhibition, and the unhappy "elephant-man" endeavoured to make a living in a similar manner in Belgium; but a sum of £50, which he had saved, was stolen by his showman and he made his way back to England in a destitute condition. He was taken in at the London Hospital; but, as Mr. Carr Gomm stated in his letter to the *Times*, the question now arises, What is to be done with him in the future? We learn from Mr. Treves that he has received piles of correspondence from the curious and from the charitable on the subject; and we trust that poor John Merrick will, through the efforts of the benevolent, be enabled to end his days in peace and privacy with a small competence.

The elephant-man is short, and lame through old disease

of the left hip joint. The integuments and the bones are deformed. The subcutaneous tissue is greatly increased in amount in certain regions, here the integument is consequently raised prominently above the surrounding skin. This tissue is very loose, so that it can be raised from the deeper parts in great folds. In the right pectoral region, at the posterior aspect of the right axilla, and over the buttocks, the affected skin forms heavy pendulous flaps.

The skin is also subject to papilloma, represented in some parts, as in the right clavicular region, by a mere roughening of the integument; over the right side of the chest, the front of the abdomen, the back of the neck, and over the right popliteal space, the growth is small; on the other hand, great masses of papillomata cover the back and the gluteal region. The eyelids, the ears, the entire left arm, nearly the whole of the front of the abdomen, the right and the left thigh, the left leg, the back of the right leg, and the penis and scrotum are free from the disease.

The deformities of the osseous system are yet more remarkable. The cranial bones are deformed and overgrown, so that the circumference of the patient's head equals that of his waist. This deformity is better shown by the woodcuts than by any verbal description. Bony exostoses spring from the frontal bone, the posterior part of the parietals, and the occipital. Irregular elevations lie between these bosses, and all these deformities are very unsymmetrical. The right superior maxillary bone is greatly and irregularly enlarged. The right side of the hard palate and the right upper teeth occupy a lower level than the corresponding parts of the left side. The nose is turned to the left, and the lips are very prominent. A connective-tissue growth was removed at the Leicester Infirmary, four years ago, from the front part of the right upper jaw.

All the bones of the right upper extremity, excepting the

clavicle and scapula, and the bones of both feet, are hypertrophied, without exostoses.

The patient can give no family history of similar deformity, but declares that his mother was knocked down by an elephant, in a circus, when bearing him. The hypertrophy of the bones existed ever since he can remember; the thickening of the skin and papillomatous growths were very trifling in degree of development during childhood. The papillary excrescences are increasing rapidly, and hypertrophy of the integuments of the right hand is causing it to become slowly crippled. The patient's general health is good.

Appendix 6

Mr. Carr Gomm's Letter To *The Times* (London), 16 April 1890, p. 6, Giving An Account Of The Death Of "The Elephant Man."

To the Editor of the Times

Sir,—In November, 1886, you were kind enough to insert in *The Times* a letter from me drawing attention to the case of Joseph Merrick, known as "the elephant man." It was one of singular and exceptional misfortune; his physical deformities were of so appalling a character that he was debarred from earning his livelihood in any other way than by being exhibited to the gaze of the curious. This having been rightly interfered with by the police of this country, he was taken abroad by an Austrian adventurer, and exhibited at different places on the Continent; but one day his exhibitor, after stealing all the savings poor Merrick had carefully hoarded, decamped, leaving him destitute, friendless, and powerless in a foreign country.

With great difficulty he succeeded somehow or other in getting to the door of the London Hospital, where, through the kindness of one of our surgeons, he was sheltered for a time. The difficulty then arose as to his future; no incurable hospital would take him in, he had a horror of the workhouse, and no place where privacy was unattainable was to be thought of, while the rules and necessities of our general hospital forbade the fund and space, which are set apart solely for cure and healing, being utilized for the maintenance of a chronic case like this, however abnormal. In this dilemma, while deterred by common humanity from evicting him again into the open street, I wrote to you, and from that moment all difficulty vanished; the sympathy of many was aroused, and, although no other fitting refuge offered, a sufficient sum was placed at my disposal, apart from the funds of the hospital, to maintain him for what did not promise to be a prolonged life. As an exceptional case the committee agreed to allow him to remain in the hospital upon the annual payment of a sum equivalent to the average cost of an occupied bed.

Here, therefore, poor Merrick was enabled to pass the three and a half remaining years of his life in privacy and comfort. The authorities of the hospital, the medical staff, the chaplain, the sisters, and nurses united to alleviate as far as possible the misery of his existence, and he learnt to speak of his rooms at the hospital as his home. There he received kindly visits from many, among them the highest in the land, and his life was not without various interests and diversions: he was a great reader and was well supplied with books; through the kindness of a lady, one of the brightest ornaments of the theatrical profession, he was taught basket making, and on more than one occasion he was taken to the play, which he witnessed from the seclusion of a private box.

He benefited much from the religious instruction of our chaplain, and Dr. Walsham How, then Bishop of Bedford, privately confirmed him, and he was able by waiting in the vestry to hear and take part in the chapel services. The present chaplain tells me that on this Easter day, only five days before his death, Merrick was twice thus attending the chapel services, and in the morning partook of the Holy Communion; and in the last conversation he had with him Merrick had expressed his feeling of deep gratitude for all that had been done for him here, and his acknowledgment of the mercy of God to him in bringing him to this place. Each year he much enjoyed a six weeks' outing in a quiet country cottage, but was always glad on his return to find himself once more "at home." In spite of all this indulgence he was quiet and unassuming, very grateful for all that was done for him, and conformed himself readily to the restrictions which were necessary.

I have given these details, thinking that those who sent money to use for his support would like to know how their charity was applied. Last Friday afternoon, though apparently in his usual health, he quietly passed away in sleep.

I have left in my hands a small balance of the money which has been sent to me from time to time for his support, and this I now propose, after paying certain gratuities, to hand over to the general funds of the hospital. This course, I believe, will be consonant with the wishes of the contributors.

It was the courtesy of *The Times* in inserting my letter in 1886 that procured for this afflicted man a comfortable protection during the last years of a previously wretched existence, and I desire to take this opportunity of thankfully acknowledging it.

I am, Sir, your obedient servant,

F. C. CARR GOMM.

House Committee Room, London Hospital, April 15.

Appendix 7

Report of the Inquest on John Merrick, *The Times* (London), 16 April 1890, p. 6.

Death Of "The Elephant Man"

An inquest on the body of Joseph Merrick, better known as the "Elephant Man," was held yesterday at the London Hospital by Mr. Baxter. Charles Merrick, of Church-gate, Leicester, a hairdresser, identified the body as that of his nephew. The deceased was 29 years of age, and had followed no occupation. From birth he had been deformed, but he got much worse of late. He had been in the hospital four or five years. His parents were in no way afflicted, and the father, an engine driver, is alive now. Mr. Ashe, house surgeon, said he was called to the deceased at 3:30 p.m. on Friday, and found him dead. It was expected that he would die suddenly. There were no marks of violence, and the death was quite natural. The man had great overgrowth of the skin and bone, but he did not complain of anything. Witness believed that the exact cause of death was asphyxia, the back of his head being greatly deformed, and while the patient was taking a natural sleep the weight of the head overcame him, and so suffocated him. The coroner said that the man had been sent round the shows as a curiosity, and when death took place it was decided as a matter of prudence to hold this inquest. Mr. Hodges, another house surgeon, stated that on Friday last he went to visit the deceased, and found him lying across the bed dead. He was in a ward specially set apart for him. Witness did not touch him. Nurse Ireland, of the Blizzard Ward, said the deceased was in her charge. She saw him on Friday morning, when he appeared in his usual health. His midday meal was taken in to him, but he did not touch it. The coroner, in summing up said there could be no doubt that death was quite in accordance with the theory put forward by the doctor. The jury accepted this view, and returned a verdict to the effect that death was due to suffocation from the weight of the head pressing on the windpipe.

Appendix 8

Report of the Death of "The Elephant Man" in *The British Medical Journal*, 19 April 1890, pp. 916-917.

Death of the "Elephant Man."

In December, 1886, a series of drawings of this afflicted person appeared in the JOURNAL. Since that date, the patient lived at the London Hospital. On Friday, April 11th, he died under circumstances which will presently be stated, having reached the age of 27, according to his relatives. His age must therefore have been overstated four years ago, as then he was believed to be 27.

He derived the name by which he was known from the proboscis-like projection of his nose and lips, together with the peculiar shape of his deformed forehead. His real name was John Merrick. He was victimised by showmen for a time; when shown in the Whitechapel Road, the police stopped the exhibition. He was afterwards exhibited in Belgium, where he was plundered of his savings. On one occasion a steamboat captain refused to take him as a passenger.

The "elephant man" was twice exhibited before the Pathological Society by Mr. Treves. His complaint was not elephantiasis, but a complication of congenital hypertrophy of certain bones, with pachydermatocele and papilloma of the skin. He was born at Leicester, and there was no family history of any similar malformation. He gave an elaborate account of a shock experienced by his mother shortly before his birth, when knocked down by an elephant at a circus. It is almost certain that he was born with enlargement of the bones of the skull, right arm, and feet. When a child his skin was simply thickened, loose, and rough. He suffered in youth from disease of the left hip-joint, which caused permanent lameness. As he grew up, papillary masses developed on his skin, especially over the back, the buttocks, and the occiput. In the right pectoral region, the posterior aspect of the right axilla, and over the buttocks, the affected skin formed heavy pendulous flaps; a considerable part of the surface of the body, including the left arm, remained free from disease.

After his exhibition at the Pathological Society, the disease rapidly advanced. The fingers became crippled by hypertrophy of their integument. His general health remained good, and he possessed a fair amount of muscular power.

Such was the condition of the patient when last described in the JOURNAL. He was then in a relatively flourishing condition, still able to go about. It remains for us to say a few words on poor Merrick's last days and death.

The bony masses and pendulous flaps of skin grew steadily. The outgrowth from the upper jaw and its integument—the so-called trunk—increased so as to render his speech more and more difficult to understand. The most serious feature, however, in the patient's illness was the increasing size of the head, which ultimately caused his death. The head grew so heavy that at length he had great difficulty in holding it up. He slept in a sitting or crouching position, with his hands clasped over his legs, and his head on his knees. If he lay down the heavy head tended to fall back and produce a sense of suffocation.

Nevertheless, the general health of the "elephant man" was relatively good shortly before his death. Early last week he was in excellent spirits, writing letters. He was out in the garden of the London Hospital on the night of April 10th. At 1:30 p.m. on Friday he was in bed (he seldom got up until the afternoon) and appeared to be perfectly well when the wardmaid brought him his dinner. Between 3 and 4 o'clock he was found dead in his bed.

Mr. Treves, to whom we are indebted for the above details, is of opinion that from the position in which the patient lay after death it would appear that the ponderous skull had fallen backwards and dislocated his neck.

An inquest was held by Mr. Wynne Baxter on the body of the "elephant man" on Tuesday last, April 15th, at the London Hospital. Mr. Ashe, house-surgeon, said he was called to the deceased at 3:30 p.m. on Friday, and found him dead. It was expected that he would die suddenly. There were no marks of violence, and the death was quite natural. The man had great overgrowth of skin and bone, but he did not complain of anything. Witness believed that the exact cause of death was asphyxia, the back of his head being greatly deformed, and while the patient was taking a natural sleep the weight of the head overcame him, and so suffocated him. The Coroner said the man had been sent round the shows as a curiosity, and when death took place it was decided as a matter of prudence to hold this inquest. Mr. Hodges, another house-surgeon, stated that on Friday last he went to visit the deceased, and found him lying across the bed, dead. He was in a ward specially set apart for him. Witness did not touch him. Nurse Ireland, of the

Blizzard Ward, said the deceased was in her charge. She saw him on Friday morning, when he appeared in his usual health. His mid-day meal was taken in to him, but he did not touch it. The Coroner, in summing up, said there could be no doubt that death was quite in accordance with the theory put forward by the doctor. The jury accepted this view, and returned a verdict to the effect "that death was due to suffocation from the weight of the head pressing on the windpipe."

We understand that the Committee of the London Hospital refused not only to permit a necropsy on the body of the "elephant man," but also declined to allow his body to be preserved. Although the verdict explains the immediate cause of his death, there is reason to believe that he was subject to cardiac disease of an uncertain nature; he was certainly troubled with bronchitis.

The circumstances under which the "elephant man" obtained the benefits of residence in the London Hospital were fully explained by Mr. Carr Gomm, chairman to the London Hospital, in a letter published in the *Times* on Wednesday. The poor fellow was grateful, intelligent, and interesting. The Princess of Wales and half the celebrities in London visited him. Ever since he entered the hospital the Princess forwarded to him yearly a Christmas card with an autograph message, whilst from time to time the Prince sent him game. Lady Dorothy Neville, Mrs. Kendal, Miss Lankester, and other ladies also showed him great kindness in a very practical manner.

The drawings [Fig. 16], kindly supplied to us by Mr. Treves, represent the "elephant man" as he appeared in 1889.

Appendix 9

Description Of The Skeleton Of "The Elephant Man"
In The Catalogue Of The Museum
Of The London Hospital Medical College

GENERALIZED HYPEROSTOSIS WITH PACHYDERMIA
The Elephant Man

The skull is the seat of extensive asymmetrical bony outgrowths affecting the frontal, right, parietal, right temporal and the right half of the occipital and sphenoidal bones. The osseous growth is not, however, accurately bounded by the sagittal plane, but extends on to the left side, especially in the frontal and occipital regions. The bony masses involve the whole frontal region except a small triangular area above and behind the left external angular process. They are very irregular, and are roughly divided into three portions by two deep longitudinal sulci. The right sulcus is practically continuous with the supra-orbital notch. The left is nearer the middle line. In the right parietal region the bosses are comparatively smooth, but several hook-like prominences arise along its lower border. The right temporo-occipital region presents an enormous mass projecting considerably on the lateral aspect and ending behind in a strong rough ledge. The external auditory meatus is a slit-like opening with a prominent anterior lip. It lies one inch below the level of the glenoid fossa. From the middle line of the occipital bone a large boss, continuous with the mass above described runs up to the back part of both parietal bones. Its left boundary is well marked off from the normal area on the left side by the skull. The right half of the base of the skull is very large, its external plate being thick and prominent. The hamular process on this side is bent strongly outwards.

The bones of the face are also affected. The lower end of the right nasal bone is prolonged into a rough prominence which encroaches on the anterior nares. The right malar bone has also a prominent boss just external to the infra-orbital foramen. The alveolar process of the maxilla projects strongly outwards at its lower part and another rough mass runs nearly horizontally inwards.

The mandible is very unequally affected. The left side presents no abnormality, but the whole of the right half is hypertrophied. The coronoid process is a stout projection reaching above the level of the floor of the orbit, and rising one inch above the condyle. The ramus is broad and is prolonged anteriorly into a rugged mass below the mental foramen. Another projection encroaches on the mouth, directing the second molar teeth inwards.

The sutures. The coronal is obliterated for an inch and a half to the left of the bregma. It is very elaborate on the right side and also at the level of the temporal ridge on the left. The sagittal is occupied posteriorly by the flattened boss above described. The lamboid is lost in the great mass on the right side.

Measurements. The greatest antero-posterior diameter

(from the root of the nose to the prominent boss in the occipital region) nine inches. The greatest transverse diameter (just in front of the external auditory meatuses) 7 1/2 inches. The circumference at the bregma 23 1/2 ins., (the right half 14 ins., and the left 9 1/2 ins.). From the middle line to the large prominence on the right side 4 7/8 ins. A corresponding measurement on the left side—2 5/8 ins. From the back of the foramen magnum to the end of the shelf-like ridge—3 3/4 ins.

The *weight* (dry and without the mandible) 4 lbs. 4 1/2 oz.

The *spine* has a well marked curvature to the left in the dorsal region, the vertebrae being also rotated. The transverse processes in the mid and upper dorsal regions are large and rough on the left side. The atlas has a large boss, nearly an inch in thickness, on the left side of the anterior arch. The left lamina of the fourth cervical vertebra is also very thick.

The pelvis is contracted and of a peculiar shape. The wings of the ilia are nearly vertical, the crests are almost straight and run in an antero-posterior plane. The left acetabulum is irregularly excavated by old tubercular disease of the hip joint. The right tuber ischii is large and prominent. Both tuberosities are directed outwards.

Measurements: Inter-spinous diameter—5 1/4 ins. Inter-cristal diameter—6 ins., Internal conjugate—4 1/2 ins.

The ulna is very large and rough. The greater sigmoid cavity is of large dimensions, extending considerably on the outer side and blending with the lesser sigmoid cavity. This, and the great prominence of the inner lip of the trochlea, throw the forearm out from the arm at an angle of 150 degrees. The head of the radius is thus thrust forward in front of the ulna.

The bones of the right carpus are large and friable. The

metacarpals and phalanges of the index, right and little fingers are of large size and soft texture. The bone of the thumb present normal characters.

Comparative weights (dry).   Right.   Left.

	Right.	Left.
Clavicle	3 1/8 oz.	1 1/4 oz.
Scapula	3	1 3/4
Humerus	6	4
Ulna	4 1/4	1 1/4
Radius	3/4	1/2

Lower Limbs. The head of the left femur ıs destroyed by old hip disease. The bone is thin and delicate. The fibula is large and thick, and its styloid process projects above the level of the head of the tibia. The shaft of the right femur is markedly bowed forward and very much thickened in its lower two-thirds. Its circumference at its widest part is 7 3/4 ins. The surface is rough and porous. The tibia is large, while the fibula is of normal proportions. The bones of the right foot are of about normal size, but they are very soft and friable.

Comparative weights.   Right.   Left.

	Right.	Left.
Femur	1 lb. 9 oz.	7 oz.
Tibia	9	6
Fibula	3/4	2

Joseph Merrick, the "Elephant Man", was born in Leicester in 1862. His parents were not in any way deformed. The appearance of the patient is well represented in the casts made after death and preserved with the skeleton. The condition was one of enormous and irregular bony hypertrophy with great overgrowth of the skin and subcutaneous tissue. A comparison of the casts with the skeleton will show that these were not always coincident; for instance, the enormous size of the right hand and foot are quite out of proportion to the hypertrophy of the bones. The deformity was congenital, but had increased considerably as the patient grew up. He was, by the hideous nature of his malady, debarred from earning a livelihood otherwise than by being exhibited. His exhibition in this country was finally prevented by the police, and he was taken on the continent and shown in various towns. Having been robbed of his savings he returned to London, and a subscription was raised whereby his maintenance in the London Hospital was provided. Here he lived for three years and a half, occupying himself with basket making. On April 11th, 1890, he died suddenly, while asleep. Death was attributed to asphyxia from the pressure of the weight of his head on the trachea.

(Treves, Sir Frederick (1923) *The Elephant Man and Other Reminiscences*).

A similar case to that of the Elephant Man is described by E. Uehlinger (1941) Archiv. für Path. Anat. (Virchow's) *308*, 396 under the title of Hyperostosis generalisata mit Pachydermie (Idiopathische familiäre generalisierte Osteophytose Friedrich-Erb-Arnold).[*] The patient was ob-

---

[*It is easy to confuse multiple neurofibromatosis with some other similar disorders. This the writer of the account of Merrick's disorder in the catalogue of the Museum of the London Hospital Medical College has done in identifying it with generalized hyperostosis with pachydermia (generalized bone overgrowth with thickening of the skin). The latter is a very different disorder from multiple neurofibromatosis. It is also hereditary, and appears to be inherited as an incomplete dominant. It usually affects every bone of the skeleton and is characterized by a uniform thickening of the bone, and simple thickening of the skin.]

served from the age of 41 until his death at the age of 55. Full measurements and weights of the bones comprising the skeleton are given.

Appendix 10

Victor Hugo, The Hunchback Of Notre Dame, And Multiple Neurofibromatosis

[The following article "Quasimodo's Diagnosis," by Lawrence M. Solomon, M.D., F.R.C.P.(C) is reprinted from the *Journal of the American Medical Association*, vol. 204, 1968, pp. 190-191. The references have been deleted.]

Quasimodo's Diagnosis

The French Romantic novelist, Victor Hugo, was fascinated by the macabre and peculiar; he was one of the few novelists of that time who reflected the earlier compassionate views expressed by Philippe Pinel for the mentally retarded and insane, yet he peopled his novels with the violent and the grotesque. Hugo's observations were often acute, and he imparted his sense of the bizarre by realistic descriptions and contrast:

Take the most hideous, repulsive, complete physical deformity; place it where it will be most striking—at the lowest, meanest, most despised stage of the social

133

edifice; light up that miserable creature from all sides with the sinister light of contrast; and then throw into him a soul, and put into that soul the purest feeling given to man . . . . The degraded creature will then transform before your eyes. The being that was small will become great; the being that was deformed will become beautiful.

It would be interesting to examine the human source material for these "hideous" creatures of Hugo, with particular attention paid to the character, Quasimodo, *Notre Dame de Paris*.

Victor's father, Joseph Sigisbert Hugo, general in the army of Joseph Bonaparte (Napoleon's brother), summoned his family to Spain in 1811. Victor was 9 years old at that time and very impressionable. At the Collège des Nobles, a school which young Victor was attending in Madrid, there was a deaf-mute, misshapen dwarf who served as a porter. This unfortunate creature, called Corcovito (the little humped one), apparently haunted the author's memory for years. Later the twisted dwarf was to appear as the wild Han in *Han d'islande* (1820), as Habibrah, the wicked jester in the melodramatic novel, *Bug Jargal* (1826), as the pitiful hunchbacked court jester, Triboulet, in *Le roi s'amuse* (the basis for the libretto of Giuseppi Verdi's opera, *Rigoletto*), and later as Gwynplaine, in *L'Homme qui rit* (1869). The character of the hunchback thus evolved in several works and reached its maturity in Quasimodo, the twisted bell ringer of Notre Dame. Hugo described Quasimodo as follows:

. . . that tetrahedron nose, that horse-shoe mouth, that little left eye stubbled up with an eyebrow of carroty bristles, while the right was completely overwhelmed and buried by an enormous wen; those irregular teeth, jagged

here and there like the battlements of a fortress; that
horny lip, over which one of those teeth protruded like
the tusk of an elephant; that forked chin; and above all
the expression . . . indeed, it might be said that his whole
person was but one grimace. His prodigious head was
covered with red bristles; between his shoulders rose an
enormous lump, which was counter-balanced by a
protuberance in front; his thighs and legs were so
strangely put together that they touched at no one point
but the knees, and seen in front, resembled two sickles
joined at the handles; his feet were immense, his hands
monstrous; but with all this deformity there was a
formidable air of strength, agility, and courage, consti-
tuting a singular exception to the external rule which
ordains that force, as well as beauty, shall result from
harmony. He looked like a giant who had been broken in
pieces and ill soldered together.

At the time of the story's main sequence, Quasimodo
was 20 years old, able to speak only with difficulty, and
deaf.

We know nothing about Quasimodo's family background. He was found wrapped in a blanket on a wooden
bed in the Church of Notre Dame (where one left
unwanted children) at about 4 years of age. He was so
small for his age when he was found, it was at first
assumed he was a newly born infant. When first appearing
before Claude Frollo, the priest who adopted him, he was
already misshapen, with crooked legs and a massive
egg-like tumor over his right eye, occluding it.

After death, his skeleton was found: "The spine was
crooked, the head depressed between the shoulders and
one leg shorter than the other. . . ."

What was wrong with Quasimodo? We know that young

Hugo, though much given to melodrama, was a superb observer—his early novels are panoramas with finely painted detail. We also know that Hugo was familiar with a real hunchback; and it is assumed by many that Quasimodo's description resulted from the novelist's remembrance of a similarly afflicted hunchback. If so, what was the probable diagnosis of this poor crumbled creature, so ugly neither man nor woman would dare look at him?

Quasimodo's disease seems to have involved three systems: the skeletal system with gross deformities, the nervous system with deafness and mental retardation, and the skin with a tumor (or tumors). It is also significant, that Quasimodo saw perfectly clearly with his unaffected eye and that he was quite strong and well adapted to his deformity. The diseases which could explain such a combination of symptoms may be divided into hereditary and nonhereditary. The nonhereditary diseases do not adequately explain either the child's thriving in the face of his abnormality or his cutaneous lesions. We must therefore conclude that Quasimodo had a hereditary condition. Of the hereditarily determined diseases, possibly the best diagnostic choice is multiple neurofibromatosis, first described by Tiselius in 1793.

Let us examine the evidence for Quasimodo's having had neurofibromatosis by comparing the bony, central nervous system, and cutaneous changes found in neurofibromatosis and those ascribed by Hugo to Quasimodo. Among the osseous manifestations of neurofibromatosis, the commonest include scoliosis; congenital bowing of the tibia, fibula, radius and ulna; and pseudoarthrosis of the legs. Crowe et al found such bone changes in 35 of the 203 patients studied. These authors also found overgrowth of bone, with enlargement of one limb, a common complication of neurofibromatosis. Spade-like hands and acromegaloid features may also be seen in the disease. Quasimodo's skeletal description corresponds, at times strikingly, to the bony changes of neurofibromatosis. Quasimodo had a tumor (Hugo used the word *verrue*, which more accurately translates as "wart") growing from his forehead and pendulously occluding his right eye. Could this lesion have been a solitary local problem? A verruca vulgaris would not likely be present from the age of 4 years to the age of 20 and achieve such great size. Dermoid cysts do occur in the region of the orbit, but they are not pendulous. A neurofibroma (molluscum pendulum) representing a systemic disease seems a better choice. His nose simply protruded from the face with its fine features missing. The chin was "forked." The mouth was in the shape of a "horseshoe," with horribly deformed teeth—one tusk-like. He had difficulty in talking. Was this lower facial deformity because of skeletal, central nervous system, or soft-tissue changes in the mouth? We are not given enough information to say with certainty, but such changes as macroteeth, jaw cysts, and soft-tissue hypertrophy are seen in neurofibromatosis. Quasimodo was mentally retarded and deaf. These two complaints are also seen in neurofibromatosis.

From the evidence presented here, it is probable that Victor Hugo's Hunchback of Notre Dame was a man suffering from neurofibromatosis and may rightly be considered the literary antecedent of another interesting character with neurofibromatosis, Sir Frederick Treves' "Elephant Man." Hugo's description of the visible aspects of his subject's skin, skeleton, and central nervous system correspond quite well to what was to be fully described 51 years later by von Recklinghausen as neurofibromatosis.

References

1. Powys, Llewellyn. *Earth Memories*. New York: W.W. Norton, 1938, p. 184.
2. Keith, Arthur. Frederick Treves. London: *Dictionary of National Biography*. Oxford University Press, 1937, pp. 856-858; *Plarr's Lives of the Fellows of the Royal College of Surgeons*. London: Simpkins, Marshall, 1930, vol. 2, p. 430.
3. "Spy," Portrait By. Men of the Day: Mr. Frederick Treves. *Vanity Fair* (London), 17 July 1900.
4. Clark-Kennedy, A.E. *The London*. London: Pitman Medical Publishing Co., 1963, 2 vols.
5. West, Jessie S. *Congenital Malformations and Birth Injuries*. New York: Association for the Aid of Crippled Children, 1954.
6. de la Mare, Walter. *Memoirs of a Midget*. London: W. Collins Sons & Co., 1921.
7. Bowlby, John. *Maternal Care and Mental Health*. Geneva: World Health Organization, 1951; John Bowlby. *Attachment and Loss*. Vol. 1, *Attachment*. New York: Basic Books, 1969; Various. *Deprivation of Maternal Care*. Geneva: World Health Organization, 1962; Casler, Lawrence, *Maternal Deprivation: A Critical Review of the Literature*. Monographs of the Society for Research in Child Development, 1961, vol. 26, no. 2; Ashley Montagu. *The Direction of Human Development*, Rev. ed. New York: Hawthorn Books, 1970.
8. Ainsworth, Mary D. "The Effects of Maternal Deprivation: A Review of Findings and Controversy in the Context of Research and Strategy," in Various. *Deprivation of Maternal Care*. Geneva: World Health Organization, 1961, pp. 97-165.
9. Plumb, J.H. "The Dwarf of Genius." *The Spectator* (London), 4 January 1957, p. 23.
10. Smith, Chard Powers. *Annals of the Poets*. New York: Scribner's, 1935, p. 484.

11. Montagu, Ashley. *Human Heredity.* 2nd ed.; New York: World Publishing Co., 1963.
12. Newman, Horatio H., Freeman, Frank N., and Holzinger, Karl J. *Twins: A Study of Heredity and Environment.* Chicago: University of Chicago Press, 1937; Newman, Horatio H. *Multiple Human Births.* New York: Doubleday, Doran & Co., 1940; Shields, James. *Monozygotic Twins.* New York: Oxford University Press, 1962; Koch, Helen C. *Twins and Twin Relations.* Chicago: University of Chicago Press, 1966; Scheinfeld, Amram. *Twins and Supertwins.* Philadelphia: Lippincott, 1967.
13. Smith, Page. *John Adams.* New York: Doubleday, 1962, vol. 1, p. 220.
14. Allport, Gordon. *Personality.* New York: Holt, 1937, p. 48.
15. Montagu. *Human Heredity.*
16. Bowlby. *Maternal Care and Mental Health,* pp. 11 and 15.
17. Various Authors. *Deprivation of Maternal Care.* 1961.
18. Spiro, Melford E. *Kibbutz: Venture in Utopia.* Cambridge: Harvard University Press, 1956; Tauber, Esther. *Molding Society to Man.* New York: Bloch Publishing Co., 1955; Weintraub, D., Lissak, M., and Azmon, Y. *Moshava, Kibbutz, and Moshav.* Ithaca: Cornell University Press, 1969.
19. Koestler, Arthur. *Thieves in the Night.* New York: Macmillan, 1946.
20. Mead, Margaret. "Discussion," in Tanner, J.M., and Inhelder, B., eds. *Discussions on Child Development.* New York: International Universities Press, vol. 2, 1956, p. 228.
21. Newton, Grant and Levine, Seymour, eds. *Early Experience and Behavior.* Springfield, Illinois: C.C. Thomas, 1968.
22. Hammond, John L. and Barbara. *The Bleak Age.* Baltimore: Penguin Books, 1947.
23. Chesney, Kellow. *The Anti-Society.* Boston: Gambit, 1970.
24. Gould, George W., and Pyle, Walter L. "Maternal Impressions," in *Anomalies and Curiosities of Medicine.* New York: Julian Press, 1956, pp. 81-85; Montagu, Ashley. "Maternal Emotions," *Prenatal Influences.* Springfield, Ill.: C.C. Thomas, 1962, pp. 169-216.
25. Montagu, Ashley. "On the Distinction Between Disease and Disorder," *Journal of the American Medical Association,* vol. 179, 1962, p. 826.
26. Von Recklinghausen, Friedrich. *Ueber die Multiplen Fibroma der Haut und ihre Beziehung zu den muliplen Neuromen.* Berlin: A. Hirschwald, 1882.
27. Crowe, F.W., Schull, W.J., and Neel, J.F. *Multiple Neurofibromatosis.* Springfield, Ill.: C.C. Thomas, 1956.
28. *Ibid.*
29. Browne, Sir Thomas. *Religio Medici.* London: Andrew Crooke, 1642.

7401

92
MER

Montagu, Ashley

The elephant man

DATE			
NOV 2 - '78	NOV 28 '89		
APR 1 78	MAY 7 '91		
MAR 31 '81	APR 26 1994		
JAN 19 '82	DEC 13 1994		
DEC 14 '82	FAC		
DEC 10 '85			
JAN 08 '86			
MAY 19 '87			
APR 29 '88			
MAY 3 '88